NOW

or

NEVER

NOW

or

NEVER

How Companies Must Change Today to Win the Battle for Internet Consumers

Mary Modahl

HarperBusiness
A Division of HarperCollins*Publishers*

This book is written as a source of information only. The information contained in this book should by no means be considered a substitute for professional advice.

All efforts have been made to ensure the accuracy of the information contained in this book as of the date published. The author and the publisher expressly disclaim responsibility for any adverse effects arising from the use or application of the information contained therein.

Note: Figures that appear in *Now or Never* are available as downloadable Power Point slides from www.forrester.com.

FIRST EDITION

Printed on acid-free paper

Library of Congress Cataloging-in-Publication Data
Modahl, Mary.
   Now or never: how companies must change today to win the battle for internet consumers / Mary Modahl.—1st ed.
      p.   cm.
   ISBN 0-06-662012-0
   1. Internet marketing.   2. Teleshopping.   3. Consumer behavior.   I. Title.
HF5415.1265.M63 2000
658.8'4—dc21

                                                                    99-049437

00 01 02 03 04 ❖/RRD 10 9 8 7 6 5

Dedicated with love to

Richard, Rebecca, and William

CONTENTS

ACKNOWLEDGMENTS

This book would never have been possible without the original ideas, moral support, and hard work of many people. First, I would like to thank Suzy Wetlaufer of the *Harvard Business Review,* whose editing improved the logic, tone, and flow of the book immeasurably, and upon whose support and friendship I relied each and every day of the process. In addition, I would like to thank Bill Bluestein from Forrester, who helped me structure the arguments and develop many of the ideas in this book. Our partnership in creating the electronic commerce research area at Forrester has been one of the most fruitful—and fun—working relationships of my career. Rob Galford from Forrester's board offered insightful feedback and a great deal of encouragement, for which I am deeply grateful.

I would like to thank Shelley Morrisette, director of quantitative research, and the entire Technographics research team at Forrester for developing the consumer insights upon which the first half of the book rests. In addition, I would like to recognize principal analyst Josh Bernoff, who created the Technographics model, and Emily Green, now Forrester's managing director in Europe, who collaborated on that project. I am grateful for the many contributions of our Technographics research partners at NPD Group, Mediamark Research, Media Metrix, and Greenfield Online—and to Rob Rubin and John Boynton, who facilitate these relationships.

Now or Never relies upon the work of nearly every member of the strategy research team at Forrester. Yet I would like to thank particularly Chris Charron, Chris Mines, Bill Doyle, James Punishill, Lisa Allen, and James McQuivey for their comments, and the on-line retail, media, business trade, leadership, and financial services teams for allowing me to draw directly upon their work.

Acknowledgments

Nicki Maraganore and Jesse Johnson each spent many hours doing research, crunching numbers, and checking for accuracy, and Eileen Roche edited the final manuscript. Without them, I could never have completed the project. Nor could I have done it without the loving care provided to me and my family by Claudia Waite, Jody Chandler, Sarah Reddick, and the teachers and parents from Nashoba Brooks School.

I would like to thank my publisher, Adrian Zackheim at HarperCollins, for his enthusiasm and persistence. Adrian imagined the book before anyone did—and he made it happen. I am also grateful to Ike Williams at Palmer and Dodge for his wise counsel.

I cannot sufficiently express my gratitude to the many Forrester clients and personal contacts who have allowed their stories to be told in this book, whether for attribution or not. They have shared their good and bad experiences on the Internet—a new territory, where no one knows all the answers. In making this brave disclosure, I feel they have advanced the industry's understanding of the Internet and its impact on business.

Finally, I give my wholehearted thanks to George Colony, president of Forrester. As leader, mentor, and friend, he has given his unqualified support to all my work endeavors, including this book.

PREFACE

There comes a moment in every emerging market when the future is no longer imaginary, when vision somehow gets a toehold in reality. The first sales ring in, actual satisfied customers emerge, and competitors have more to talk about than just plans. For Internet commerce, that moment came in the fourth quarter of 1998, when holiday season revenues at Web sites rose to four times what they had been the year before. Once the results were in, everyone suddenly realized that the Internet was going to be a big deal—that whole industries would be restructured as a result of electronic commerce and that consumer behavior would change forever.

People weren't always convinced the Internet would live up to its hype. I remember giving a breakfast speech in New York just two years before to a group of about fifty company executives. The speech was called "The Internet Economy," and it argued that media, retail, and financial services would be among the first industries to be affected by the Internet. As I spoke, I looked around at the audience, trying to sense whether the message resonated. It didn't. With one or two exceptions, the faces around the room were blank. Adjusting, I added some humor and a couple of anecdotes that I hoped would help the audience open up to what I was trying to share with them.

But when the presentation ended and the question time began, I could see that these people simply were not prepared to hear the message of the speech. A hard-boiled skepticism dominated their thoughts. For these executives, the Internet was nothing more than some kind of freaky sideshow. This assumption showed in their questions, which focused almost entirely on the obstacles to Internet adoption among consumers—slow connection speeds, security concerns, and the high price of computers.

This year, speaking at a marketing conference held on board the *Queen Elizabeth II* to an audience roughly the same in composition but ten times larger, I had an entirely different experience. By mid-1999, it was clear to all that the Internet would cause the biggest business battle of our time. In the hallways, people spoke of "being Amazoned"—a new slang verb that describes the process by which an Internet start-up such as Amazon uses a high stock price to buy its way into your market and then offers the same products as you, at half the price. Over lunch, these executives, who represented mostly traditional companies, traded notes about how to get their CEO to act before it was too late.

Stepping onto the stage for a pre-dinner talk about Internet consumers, I surveyed the room, taking in the mood. This time, the group looked panic-stricken. It was as if they woke up one day and were told, "You've been at war, and your side just lost. Pack up your belongings, because you don't live here anymore." I realized the extent to which the skyrocketing IPOs of new Internet competitors had shaken the confidence of executives at even the best companies.

But I was there to tell them—and in this book I will argue—that the battle is far from over. It took two decades for the Internet to evolve from a military project into a commercial network, and a full five years after that for electronic commerce of any magnitude to emerge. As I write in 1999, we stand barely more than one year into a ten-year transition in the way consumers shop and save. In reality, the battle is just beginning.

The winners in this transition—and the losers—will come from the ranks of both traditional companies and dotcoms. For nothing guarantees *any* company a ticket to the Internet's future. That ticket has to be earned each and every day over the next ten years. In the end, only those companies that can offer Internet consumers real value at a competitive price and still turn a profit will survive.

My interest in Internet strategy developed out of my work at Forrester® Research, which advises corporate clients in the area of electronic commerce. This work began as far back as 1989, when I became director of network technology research at Forrester. But it was in 1992 that I first realized that the Internet would emerge as a kind of public utility—connecting people and companies in a giant network. Another group at Forrester was working on the idea that technology would change popular culture, and others theorized that computing would make its way out of companies and into the hands of millions of individuals.

Those ideas were so outlandish at the time that we called them, collectively, "the New Bubble." But they also resonated enough that we decided to devote a research team to exploring them. So in early 1994, when Internet browsers were still used only by academics and Al Gore had just made his first Information Superhighway speech, a team of us split off from corporate technology research and formed the electronic commerce practice, which today accounts for most of Forrester's business.

As an industry analyst and consultant, I have witnessed firsthand the struggles of managers at both start-ups and traditional companies to establish successful businesses on the Internet. Over the last five years, I have advised dozens of different companies on Internet strategy. Just as important, I have had the opportunity to test new ideas through Forrester's research. Each year, Forrester conducts more than 125,000 interviews with consumers to explore why they buy and use technology and more than 10,000 interviews with company managers to understand how businesses thrive on technology change. In addition, Forrester's research teams track the progress of new software and hardware from university and company labs to commercial application. This primary research has been a tremendous resource to draw upon when advising clients, and it also forms the basis for this book.

In the next two hundred pages, I am going to argue that the battle for Internet consumers is still being fought, and it can be won by either traditional players or start-up companies. The struggle is not over. Yet time *is* running short. Traditional companies won't be able to hide from the Internet much longer—they're going to have to get in the ring and fight to keep their consumers. Start-up Internet companies, which have grown prodigiously while generating ever larger losses, must soon begin to turn a profit.

As Internet commerce ceases to be an imaginary future and turns out, in fact, to be a catalyst for change throughout the economy, the competition will become all too real. Companies that intend to win in this environment must set a course that will enable them to survive the intense competition of the battle years. This book sets forth the strategic imperatives for winning on the Internet, but it's up to each individual company to act on them quickly. In the battle for Internet consumers, it's *Now or Never*.

INTRODUCTION

We have entered a time when doing business over the Internet is no longer a novelty but a necessity. Electronic sales to consumers will pass $20 billion in 1999, and Forrester and others project a more than sixfold increase in the next few years (see Figure 1).

In addition, Internet commerce affects business far beyond the scope of actual sales, as start-ups challenge long-standing business practices in many consumer industries. Traditional company managers note alarming trends, such as:

- **New pricing models that undermine existing revenues.** In many cases, Internet companies bet that they can lower prices and make up revenues on volume. In financial services, for example, Internet companies charge individual investors low flat-rate fees instead of variable commissions on trading.

- **Higher customer-service expectations**. Internet businesses are open twenty-four hours a day, seven days a week, and they allow consumers to help themselves to information about products before buying. Some of the busiest hours for these new companies occur during workweek breaks, when consumers at the office take ten minutes to buy a gift or plan a weekend away.

- **New ways to distribute products**. Internet companies build their businesses around home delivery—even in markets where home delivery has never existed before. This has caught traditional companies, which focus on consumers' in-store experience, off guard. For example, traditional booksellers believed that people wanted to touch a book before buying it. And grocers thought that consumers would never trust a service to

(billions)	1999	2000	2001	2002	2003	2004	% of total 2004 retail
Total U.S. revenue	20.3	39.2	65.1	102.7	145.5	187.9	7%
Total convenience	7.0	13.9	23.3	40.2	55.4	72.5	9%
Media	3.6	5.5	7.4	10.1	11.1	12.6	22%
Event tickets	0.3	0.7	1.2	1.9	2.9	3.9	14%
Apparel	1.6	3.6	6.6	14.7	20.2	27.1	9%
Gifts and flowers	0.7	1.0	1.8	2.9	3.9	4.7	12%
Household goods	0.3	0.6	1.2	2.1	3.6	5.8	8%
Recreation	0.6	2.6	5.1	8.5	13.7	18.5	6%
Total researched	11.4	21.1	33.8	48.4	65.9	78.8	8%
Leisure travel	7.8	14.0	20.7	26.0	29.4	32.1	12%
Automobiles	—	0.4	1.8	4.5	12.2	16.6	4%
Electronics	3.2	5.8	9.7	15.3	20.2	24.2	16%
Housewares	0.4	1.0	1.6	2.6	4.1	5.9	6%
Total replenishment	1.8	4.1	7.9	14.1	24.2	36.6	4%
Food and beverage	0.5	1.1	2.5	5.0	10.8	16.9	3%
Health and beauty	0.5	1.2	2.1	3.8	6.3	10.3	5%
Miscellaneous	0.8	1.8	3.4	5.2	7.0	9.4	14%

Not all figures add up due to rounding

Source: Forrester Research, Inc.

Figure 1   U.S. On-line Retail Projections by Category

choose their family's food. In both cases, past experience led to the wrong conclusion.

- **Unexpected market opportunities**. Because the Internet connects people across very wide distances at extremely low cost, start-ups can dream up services that literally were never possible before. Take, as an example, consumer-to-consumer auctions, which bring together millions of people to offer or bid on hundreds of thousands of items daily.

- **High rates of entry—even in very staid markets**. Conservative industries such as newspaper classified advertising, which had not seen a significant entrant in decades, find themselves challenged by newcomers.

These trends suggest that even giant consumer companies can no longer ignore the possible impact of the Internet. Traditional companies must take part in the new market and defend themselves against the incursion of the start-ups.

The stage is set for the battle for Internet consumers—a conflict that will span more than ten years as companies adjust their strategies to take advantage of the Internet's ability to let consumers buy anytime, anywhere. On one side of this battle stand the established corporations—companies and brands that people have known since childhood. On the other stand the "dotcoms," start-ups that believe they can offer consumers a better deal and become a household name in the process.

The battlefield is uneven. Start-ups, with their Internet birthright, have the advantage. Being small, newer companies can move quickly, and their entire business revolves around a single focus. In addition, start-ups have had easy access to venture funding and more risk-tolerant investors than traditional companies. But most important, the dotcoms have nothing to lose if the old ways of doing business fade away.

Traditional companies have developed a core of well-understood business practices. Although this core is valuable, it also creates a gravity field, trapping the company by continually pulling it back toward the way it has always done business. This gravity can make it amazingly difficult for traditional companies to understand fully what changes are possible in their industries. Even when they do understand, it is tough for them to act. So many old, comfortable habits must be broken in order to compete on the Internet that, in truth, few traditional companies have been able to do it well.

The fact that smaller, venture-backed companies have done better on the Internet so far has led many people to conclude that traditional companies have no chance of winning the battle for Internet consumers. But this black-or-white conclusion fails to take account of the fact that traditional companies are only now beginning to fight back. With a few exceptions, start-ups have not yet faced any significant competition for their share of the Internet market.

Moreover, the early success of the start-ups has actually created the single biggest problem they face. As the start-ups grew and investor excitement about their prospects mounted, these barely formed entities found that they could offer public stock without being profitable. As a result, most of the rewards for growing an Internet business from scratch have already been reaped—in advance. Regardless of where the market heads next, the far-too-fast run-up in the value of tiny Internet companies in early 1999 spawned a cancer among the dotcoms. Getting rich quick is now a built-in expectation of start-up employees—a situation that makes it very difficult for a dotcom leader to grow a lasting enterprise.

Traditional companies also bring significant strengths to the battle for Internet consumers. First and foremost, consumers trust the companies they have done business with for decades. This familiarity will turn out to be an important advantage as Internet commerce spreads from the bolder consumers who first got on the Internet in the mid-1990s to the more reluctant mainstream. The more wary consumers are, the more that knowing the brands helps them get on-line and shop. In addition, traditional companies can span on-line and off-line venues. It is tough for any start-up to match the physical presence and consumer awareness of an established company that owns a chain of stores, or runs billboard, TV, and radio advertising.

In the end, the winners—and the losers—in the battle of the Internet will include both traditional companies and start-ups. Among the winners will be traditional companies that can learn to compete on Internet terms and start-ups that manage their way sanely through the turbulence of high growth and inflated expectations. Traditional companies that fail to understand the new environment will be left behind, and start-ups that keep losing money won't survive.

AN OVERVIEW OF *NOW OR NEVER*

This book is for traditional managers and start-up leaders alike. It examines what companies must do to win the battle for Internet consumers and to create long-term value in an Internet business. Rather than handicap the dotcoms versus the traditional companies, this book focuses on what *every* company must do to emerge as a winner on the Internet. By the end, regardless of which type of company you represent, you will have a clear sense of what it will take to succeed.

The Internet changes many of the rules of doing business—and this book will look carefully at those changes. But the most important rules, such as "know your customer," "add real value," and "differentiate from competitors," haven't really changed at all. The same frameworks that managers have used to understand business all along still apply.

Both traditional companies and Internet start-ups must accomplish three objectives in order to ultimately succeed. *Now or Never* is organized around these imperatives.

1: **Understand Internet consumers**. The early adopters of the Internet are far different from the mainstream consumers who follow. As the Internet spreads to a broader cross section of households, the tastes and requirements of the average Internet consumer will change. Only companies that understand the different types of Internet consumers will be able to target the right people with the right products, services, and messages.

2: **Exploit Internet business models**. The Internet makes markets more competitive because buyers and sellers can find each other more easily. Companies must understand how revenues, costs, and value creation are affected by this heightened competitiveness.

3: **Defy the gravity of the old ways of doing business**. As Internet businesses expand, age-old management challenges such as continuous technology change, sales-channel conflict, funding, organization, and leadership take on new forms. At the outset of the battle of the Internet, traditional companies have far more gravity to contend with than start-ups do. Yet every organization, especially those that formed around the World Wide Web, must expect continued rapid technology change, and with it, new ways of doing business. The Web as we know it is not the final word from the computer industry.

PART ONE: UNDERSTANDING INTERNET CONSUMERS

Part One of *Now or Never* unravels the mystery of why consumers buy on the Internet. I am going to share with you a very important discovery that we have made at Forrester Research: When it comes to determining whether consumers will or won't go on the Internet, how much they'll spend, and what they'll buy, demographic factors such as age, race, and gender don't matter anywhere near as much as the consumers' *attitudes toward technology*.

Forrester's researchers first began to realize the importance of technology attitudes in mid-1997. At the time, we were writing a report on the personal computer market. PCs cost an average of almost $2,000 apiece back then, and partly for that reason, only about 40 percent of American households had them. Yet some homes had more than one. In fact, some were onto their third and even fourth PC. We wanted to know if all the growth in the industry would come from this same 40 percent of households or if the rest of the population would eventually start buying computers, too. And if so, at what price?

As we analyzed mountains of data about PC purchasing patterns, we noticed that college students and senior citizens had very distinctive PC buying and usage patterns. College students saw their PCs as a necessity for school as well as a source of entertainment. They bought the latest, most powerful PC they could afford, and they often added on graphics accelerators and joysticks to play games. Senior citizens, who were far less likely to buy computers overall, bought standard models and viewed them as fancy typewriters.

But when we looked at the remaining category—the twenty-five-to fifty-five-year-olds that make up the majority of the population—we found that age and life interests could not explain PC buying behavior on a consistent basis. If you took three demographically identical families, you would find one family that liked its first PC so much it bought a second one, another that owned a PC but never used it, and another with no plans to buy a PC at any price.

We began to think that maybe something else—something beyond age, income, or number of children—was driving consumer behavior. Maybe people's actions were determined by their *attitude toward technology itself.* Perhaps some consumers were inherently *optimists* about technology, believing that it could help them in their lives, while others were *pessimists* who were afraid of using computers, hostile toward them, or simply indifferent.

Over the next eighteen months, Forrester, with the help of our partners at NPD Group, mounted a massive research effort to test this hypothesis and, if it proved to be correct, to identify which consumer activities were most affected by attitudes toward technology. When all was said and done, the research project involved questionnaires, focus groups, and interviews with more than 250,000 North American consumers—the largest study of consumer technology adoption ever conducted in North America.[1]

When the results were in, we found that attitude toward technology indeed affects consumer PC buying more than any other factor. In fact, it turns out that consumers' attitudes influence their adoption of all kinds of digital technology—including Internet connections, cellular telephones, and digital TV. Not only that, these latent beliefs also affect how quickly consumers will shop on-line, how much money they will spend, and how fast they will progress from merely looking at products on-line to actually buying them.

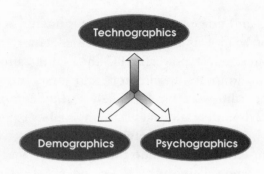

Source: Forrester Research, Inc.

Figure 2 Technographics Segments Consumers in the Internet Economy

Forrester used the information we gathered to create a new tool for understanding consumers. We call our tool Technographics because it is a system of classifying consumers, just like demographics or psychographics. Yet unlike these other schema, Technographics is custom-made for the Internet economy. Rather than separating consumers by age or lifestyle, this new system segments people according to their behavior as *digital* consumers (see Figure 2).

Technographics segments consumers according to their attitude toward technology, their motivation to use technology, and their ability to afford technology (see Figures 3 and 4).

The chapters of Part One impart the most significant findings of the Technographics consumer study.[2] Chapter 1 examines the roots of technology optimism and pessimism in consumers. Using this information and the self-assessment test in chapter 2, companies will be able to determine if their existing consumer base is composed mainly of early adopters, mainstream consumers, or laggards.

Chapters 3, 4, and 5, respectively, look at each of these three groups of consumers. Chapter 3 identifies early adopters and outlines the key messages and marketing strategies that succeed with these consumers. Chapter 4 presents Technographics research about the mainstream—a vast group of more than eighty-eight million people—identifying which mainstreamers prefer doing business with traditional companies and which ones are open to start-ups. Chapter 5 looks at laggards—consumers who have too few resources to buy PCs

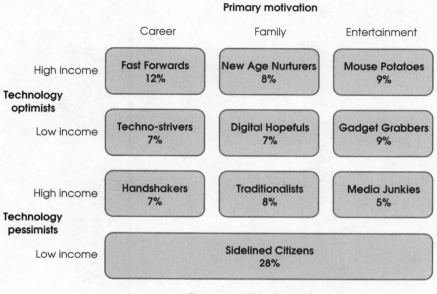

Percent of 204 million U.S. adults

Source: Forrester Research, Inc.

Figure 3 Consumer Technographics Segments in the U.S.

and lack sufficient interest to learn about technology. While it may seem that such consumers can be safely ignored, laggards make up 28 percent of the population of North America. Traditional mass-market companies such as Wal-Mart, Nike, and Kellogg's must take these consumers into account when constructing an Internet strategy.

PART TWO: EXPLOITING INTERNET BUSINESS MODELS

In Part Two, *Now or Never* moves on to the Internet business model imperative. In chapter 6 we'll look at how the Internet is changing supply and demand, moving consumer industries toward a new competitive environment that Forrester calls *Dynamic Trade*. The changes caused by Dynamic Trade are at once so simple and so profound that their full impact can be difficult to grasp.

Digital Hopefuls *n. pl.*

1) family-oriented technology lovers with low incomes;
2) promising future market for low-cost PCs

Fast Forwards *n. pl.*

1) high-income, career-oriented technology adopters;
2) driven careerists, time-strapped, often in dual-income households;
3) leading users of business and productivity software

FAST FORWARD

Gadget Grabbers *n. pl.*

1) lower-income consumers focused on tech-based entertainment;
2) Nintendo/Sega gamers;
3) buyers of low-cost, high-tech toys

Handshakers *n. pl.*

1) successful professionals with low technology tolerance;
2) dealmakers and executives

HANDSHAKER

Media Junkies *n. pl.*

1) high-income, entertainment-oriented individuals—not PC-savvy;
2) visual consumers
3) TV lovers
4) early adopters of satellite TV

Mouse Potatoes *n. pl.*

1) high-income, entertainment-focused technology consumers;
2) those dedicated to interactive entertainment, especially on a PC

MOUSE POTATO

New Age Nurturers *n. pl.*

1) affluent believers in technology for family and education;
2) least-served group of future technology consumers

Sidelined Citizens *n. pl.*

1) low-income technophobes;
2) the least receptive audience for any technology;
3) technology laggards

Techno-strivers *n. pl.*

1) up-and-coming believers in technology for career advancement;
2) students or young professionals;
3) of low-income segments, this group has the highest percentage of computer ownership

Traditionalists *n. pl.*

1) high-income, family-minded individuals suspicious of technology;
2) Midwestern and small-town dwellers with little technology beyond VCRs

Source: Forrester Research, Inc.

Figure 4   Definitions of Technographics Segments

Consider, for example, the way minivans are sold today. Somewhere in Texas, at the intersection of two crosstown highways, stands a four-acre square of asphalt where a dealer displays the models currently on sale from Chevrolet. In the far corner are parked five minivans, all green. In walks a couple with their hearts set on a white minivan.

Now this dealer has a salesman, an ambitious young fellow whose sole job is to convince this couple that what they really want is a green minivan, because the dealer isn't getting a white one in until next month. Luckily, the young salesman is so talented that by the end of the month he has not only convinced *this* couple to buy a green minivan but has sold the remaining four.

The dealer is thrilled. He didn't expect to sell the green minivans anytime soon, since consumers vastly prefer white in this Texas town. He gladly pays the salesman fifteen hundred dollars in commission. Back in Detroit, the data comes in: Green minivans are hot in Texas. Make some more![3]

The lack of information in the selling system results in a loss of value for both the consumers and the manufacturer in this scenario. What would happen if the consumers used the Internet to find their car? For starters, the couple would never even go out to the crosstown dealer because they would know in advance that he doesn't have what they want. Instead, they would locate a dealer who could supply a white minivan. Next, because the information about sales is captured electronically, the manufacturer would not make more *green* minivans; it would make more *white* ones. The salesman and the dealer would lose out. Fewer minivan buyers would require such a hard sell in a market with better information flow.

This story shows the two main effects of the Internet on competition, which will be covered in chapter 6:

1. An increase in the *apparent supply*. The Internet makes it possible for consumers to locate other sources for the same products they once bought only from local retailers. This means that when consumers "shop around," they can con-

sider many more possibilities than they could in the past, when they had to drive or wait for a catalog.

2. The requirement for companies to respond to *current demand*. In the past, companies forecasted demand in order to plan production and reviewed what was sold after the fact. The Internet makes it possible for the first time to see what consumers are buying today—in other words, what the demand for a product is right now.

Dynamic Trade will require both traditional companies and start-ups to make significant investments in technology and distribution. In the end, the companies that will do best in the Dynamic Trade environment will be those that grow to a large enough scale to measure and respond to supply and demand changes in the marketplace.

Chapter 7 brings the discussion of changes in supply and demand down to the level of individual businesses. This chapter looks at how start-up companies attack the revenue mix that has defined traditional consumer industries. Doing so allows the start-ups to gain market share.

Chapter 8 wraps up Part Two of *Now or Never* with a look at how companies create value on the Internet. We'll look at how Internet companies are replacing brands based on projected images with brands based on on-line experiences. We'll examine the role of consumer information in creating those brand experiences—and assess which types of customer information can legitimately be used for selling and which are taboo. Finally, we'll consider the role of physical distribution in the Internet economy and how companies can create a unique value by providing the service that all Internet companies need but few do well.

PART THREE: DEFYING THE GRAVITY OF THE OLD WAYS OF DOING BUSINESS

The third part of *Now or Never* identifies the impediments to Internet success that traditional companies face. First among these impediments is the challenge that traditional companies, and in fact many start-ups too, face in managing technology change. The Internet has increased the level of dependence of consumer businesses upon technology, and consequently, companies need a new level of competence at technology management. Chapter 9 sets forth some of the best practices in this area.

Many companies avoid selling on the Internet mainly because they fear that doing so would cause a backlash among their retail partners. Being new, start-ups have not had to grapple with the paralyzing reality of angry retailers, dealers, franchisees, and brokers. Chapter 10 outlines a strategy for managing Internet distribution from the manufacturer's point of view.

Chapter 11 looks at the challenge of funding, organizing, and leading an Internet venture. In this area, start-ups have once again had an easier path than have most traditional companies. Look inside a dotcom you'll find a CEO who understands the Internet, an organization that shares a vision for capitalizing on the Internet, and a source of funding that allows the company to make a lot of mistakes trying. Inside a traditional company, you typically find a CEO who spends a tiny fraction of his or her time on Internet-related issues, an e-commerce group separated in mission and culture from the rest of the organization, and a source of funding that is both insufficient and worried.

No book can solve the kinds of problems that a lack of leadership creates, but in chapter 11, *Now or Never* at least identifies the antigravity strategies that have worked best in traditional companies. Chapter 12 wraps up with a summary and a look at why some companies—and individuals—end up prevailing in markets that are changing fast. Suffice it to say that only those companies with the will to win are going to be able to compete with the dotcoms.

THE VIEW THROUGH THE CRYSTAL BALL

"Yes, yes, yes," you think. "Now tell me what will happen. Who will win and who will lose?"

Personally, I expect that in every consumer industry, at least one or two of the traditional leaders will fail to make the transition to the Internet. Likewise, winners will emerge in every sector from among the start-up companies. Forrester regularly handicaps individual players in most e-commerce segments, and I welcome you to compare notes on the current standings at www.forrester.com.

Yet I think it only fair to say that the winners and the losers in the battle for Internet consumers have yet to be determined. Many of the early hotshot companies will fall prey to unrealistic expectations on the part of their investors, employees, and consumers. Some of the least involved traditional companies will at some point pivot toward the Internet with astonishing impact.

One thing is clear: The time for waiting and watching is past. The Internet is quickly moving from being merely a curiosity to being really useful. Before long, many consumers will see the Internet as a necessity. Any company that wants to be a player on the Internet will have to have its position staked out before that happens. Staking out a position begins with targeting the right consumers, and that is where we'll turn in Part One of *Now or Never*.

PART 1

Understanding Internet Consumers

CHAPTER 1

Why Consumers Buy On-line

Understanding why, when, and how different people shop on-line is the first step in winning the battle for Internet consumers. Unfortunately, it is nearly impossible, on the surface, to tell which consumers will become avid on-line shoppers, which ones won't, and most important, why.

Take me and my friend Sue as examples. In the eyes of the conventional market researcher, we look exactly the same. We are both in our late thirties, married for ten years to men who work in finance, and residents of the same Boston suburb. She has three children and I have two, but all of our children are between the ages of three and eight. We attended similar colleges, and we even drive the same kind of car.

But when it comes to on-line shopping, count me in and Sue out. I love shopping on-line. Sure, it took me some time to figure out how to get around the Web and to learn which sites had the products I wanted. But, oh, the joy of not having to go to the store! No driving! No parking! No dragging my kids through the mall, bribing them to stay quiet and remain at my side. I am now a devotee of on-line shopping for toys, clothing, books, music, videos, and even airline tickets.

Not only do I shop on-line, I use the Internet to make my life more efficient and productive in myriad ways. When my husband and I decided to redo the kitchen, I researched appliances on-line. I used the Internet to find the perfect dude ranch for an upcoming vacation. As a special treat for my son's sixth birthday party, I located an on-line candy wholesaler and ordered a twenty-four-pack retail display of Pez candy dispensers in the shape of *Star Wars* characters.

I like on-line shopping so much that I am constantly urging my friends to try it. But Sue will have none of it. She doesn't shop on-line at all. In fact, Sue and her husband don't even have a PC in their house. They say they'll probably get one soon "for the children." But even then, Sue doesn't think she'll use it much or go shopping on-line. "I know where I want to buy everything," she explains. "And I have good relationships with my travel agent, the sales people in the shops where I buy clothing, and my local bookstore. I like the personal service they give me. Shopping on-line is a good idea for some people, I guess, but it feels like it would be more of a hassle for me."

For executives trying to figure out what the Internet means for their business, the fact that Sue and I act so differently causes no end of frustration. These executives want to know: Will *all* consumers begin shopping on the Internet? How fast? Which ones will and which ones won't? This information will drive critical investments in people and technology, not to mention overall strategy. But nothing in the traditional arsenal of market research or management experience helps businesspeople *predict* how consumers will move to on-line shopping.

Even the reliable old war horse of market research—demographics—isn't helping. When the executives at Toys "R" Us look at the demographics of their industry, mainly young parents, they see that fewer than 10 percent currently shop on-line. What the data cannot help them see is how many *will* shop on-line, and when. Is it just another 2 or 3 percent? Or will it be 30 percent in 2003? For the record, Forrester's research suggests that the number is closer to 60 percent.

How did we come up with that number? At Forrester, we have spent the past three years identifying the key drivers of consumer behavior in relation to technology. This research unearthed the traits that make a person most likely to become an on-line shopper.

This information is crucial because only those companies that know *which* consumers will go on-line will thrive on the Internet. Companies that wait to find out won't have a fighting chance. By the time consumers have settled into their ultimate on-line behavior patterns, the battle will be over.

Return, then, to Sue and me. If we share so many traits, what causes our on-line buying habits to diverge so markedly? The answer, most simply stated, is that we have different *attitudes* toward technology. I am a *technology optimist,* and Sue is a *technology pessimist.* I am willing, in fact I am eager, to spend time learning to use new technology. The effort doesn't frustrate or anger me—I see it as an opportunity to improve my life. I even think it's sort of fun. Sue, by contrast, is totally indifferent to technology. She can't see any reason to take the time from her busy day to figure out how to transfer all her personal information into a Palm Pilot. Her life works just fine without it. In fact, at times, Sue thinks technology might be doing more harm than good in this world. "It's dehumanizing," she told me once.

Now let's look at the entire population. *Our research shows that 52 percent of people are optimists; the rest are pessimists.*[1] That means that a little over half the public is marching happily toward on-line shopping, while the other half resists buying a PC and connecting to the Internet. Not only that, but the pessimists who *do* buy a PC because their children need it for school or because they must use a computer for work are far slower to shop on-line than optimists are.

Understanding the role of technology optimism in the development of electronic commerce has been the thrust of Forrester's Technographics research over the past three years. In total, we have interviewed more than a quarter of a million consumers to understand what drives them to shop on-line. The result of this research is a tool that can help any company understand which consumers they should target on-line. Technographics classifies consumers according to the three factors that most influence a person's behavior (see Figure 1).

1: **Attitude toward technology.** First we ask, Is this person a technology optimist or a pessimist? To understand whether indi-

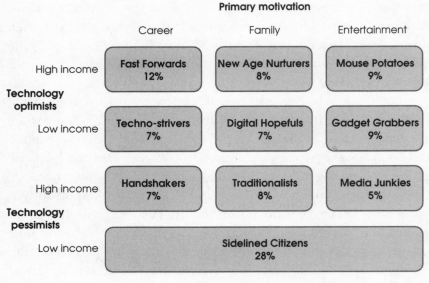

Primary motivation

	Career	Family	Entertainment
Technology optimists — High income	Fast Forwards 12%	New Age Nurturers 8%	Mouse Potatoes 9%
Technology optimists — Low income	Techno-strivers 7%	Digital Hopefuls 7%	Gadget Grabbers 9%
Technology pessimists — High income	Handshakers 7%	Traditionalists 8%	Media Junkies 5%
Technology pessimists — Low income	Sidelined Citizens 28%		

Percent of 204 million U.S. adults

Source: Forrester Research, Inc.

Figure 1   Consumer Technographics Segments in the U.S.

viduals are optimists or pessimists, Forrester has developed a set of questions that delve into *how people feel* about technology. People who score high on this Technographics scale are classified as optimists; low-scoring individuals are pessimists. The Technographics scale is continuous, but the research shows that technology polarizes people. Individuals either like technology or they don't.

2: **Income.** The amount of money a consumer has to spend strongly influences his or her on-line shopping behavior. In Technographics, we call people who earn more than $40,000 a year high income, while those earning less are classed as low income. We drew the line at $40,000 because a family that must cover taxes, housing, food, clothing, and transportation at this income level finds it tough to afford a computer.

3: **Motivation to use technology.** Beyond the questions of whether a person feels favorably toward technology and has enough money to afford it, there is a question of *motivation*. Why bother? Technographics gets behind consumers' behavior to understand what drives them to act.

HOW CONSUMERS FORM TECHNOLOGY ATTITUDES

Like all attitudes, people's attitude toward technology takes shape as they grow up. The experiences that young people have through educators, family, and friends influence them deeply. As people enter their twenties, however, their beliefs tend to solidify, becoming less and less open to outside influence. Once formed, the beliefs that define a personality remain fairly constant. So it is with technology optimism and pessimism.

That is why we see a clear generational divide between children and their parents and teachers when it comes to computers. Children revel in the digital technology that surrounds them—feeding their Tamagotchis at recess and learning phonics at home with Reader Rabbit. Parents may yearn for a return to wooden blocks and Raggedy Ann, but children just aren't interested—"What can it *do*?" they ask. Teachers also have difficulty accepting new educational toys. Their reactions to these innovations range from timidly hopeful to aggressively hostile. As adults, teachers and parents have far more difficulty accepting new technology than their children do.

People who learn about a particular technology in their youth appear to remain open to further refinements of the same technologies. But as adults they do not assimilate radical innovations very well. So while members of our grandparents' generation witnessed the advent of the automobile and adjusted to a wide range of new transportation in their lifetimes, very few have adopted computers. It seems that as all people age, they slowly become pessimistic about new technologies.

Technographics reveals this basic generational pattern: People over sixty-five are overwhelmingly pessimistic about computer technology. Baby boomers, who grew up in a time when computers

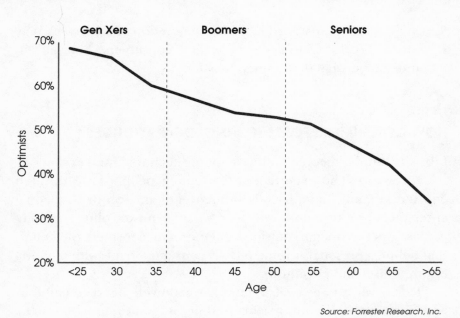

Source: Forrester Research, Inc.

Figure 2 Technology Optimism Decreases with Age

existed but were not part of most people's daily lives, are almost evenly divided between technology optimists and pessimists. People between the ages of twenty and thirty-five were first exposed to computers as far back as grade school and tend to be much more optimistic (see Figure 2).

So technology optimists tend to be young, and pessimists, old. Yet two factors can alter behavior, and ultimately attitudes, well into adulthood. The first is exposure to technology at work. A comparison of technology optimism in the largest fifty cities in the United States with PC use at work clearly shows that correlation. In places where many people use PCs at work, there are more optimists (see Figure 3).

This could reflect either that optimists have a propensity to move to jobs where technology is used or that the use of PCs at work makes a person more optimistic—we cannot be sure which. What is clear, though, is that the two go hand in hand.

The possible impact of workplace experience on technology attitudes is most noticeable among boomer women. Those who work in

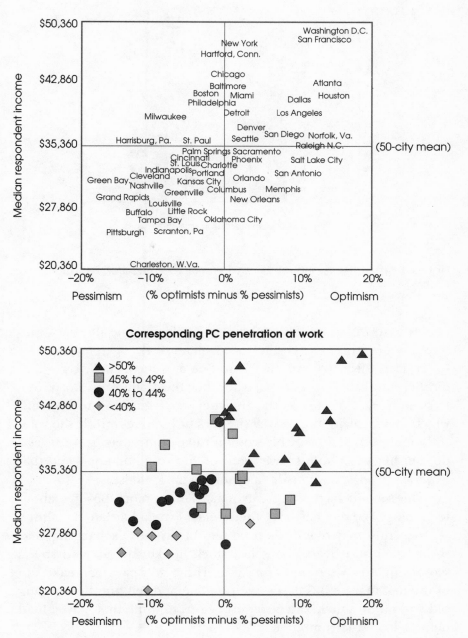

Source: Forrester Research, Inc.

Figure 3 Technographics Segmentation of the 50 Largest U.S. Cities

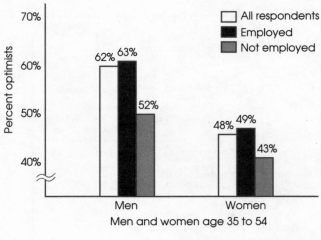

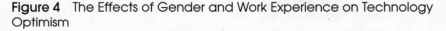

Source: Forrester Research, Inc.

Figure 4 The Effects of Gender and Work Experience on Technology Optimism

offices tend to be optimistic about technology, while the ones who stay at home tend to be pessimistic (see Figure 4).

In fact, this is true of my friend Sue and me as well. I work, as did Sue until three years ago, when her third child was born. She left the workforce just as the Internet was beginning to take off, which may explain in part why she sees little value in it. If she were still employed, Sue probably wouldn't like computers as much as I do, but her work would have required her to go on-line—and that experience *might* have made her more of an optimist.

The second factor that can make adults more positive about technology is the behavior of their peers. Even a hardened technology pessimist may relent when he sees his friends exchanging electronic mail and hears about live stock market quotes and sports scores on-line. When his Saturday-morning golf partners make fun of the fact that he has never been on-line and tell him he's getting old and out of touch, the pessimist begins to think that maybe he'd better try out the computer.

Work requirements and peer pressure can cause pessimists to adopt technology, and over time their attitudes may change. But it won't happen quickly. Across the entire consumer population, mass attitude changes move at glacial speeds. It will be more than a decade before most of the women who have stayed home to care for their children return to the workforce, and twenty years before the children who amaze us with their openness to technology reach economic maturity. I would argue that, for businesses whose long-range plans typically extend for five years, technology optimism and pessimism can be considered fixed attributes of their consumer base.

THE IMPACT OF INCOME ON TECHNOLOGY ADOPTION

There is a widely held misconception that technology appeals only to people with high incomes. In reality, 40 percent of affluent individuals are technology pessimists. In addition, many people with low incomes, such as college students and young families, can be counted among the most optimistic technology consumers.

The misconception arises because people with high incomes buy more of everything, including technology, than low-income people do. High-income households control more than three-quarters of the total personal disposable income in the United States, and that wealth is distributed across both technology optimists and pessimists (see Figure 5).

Pessimists with a lot of money buy computers, cell phones, and other digital gadgetry as part of a higher overall spending level—even though they don't particularly like technology and don't use it very readily.

We all know people like this. In fact, my father is one of them. After years of prodding from his colleagues, he finally got a PC and hooked it up to the Internet. It took him ages to get an e-mail account, and I can't remember him sending me more than one message. But my father's overall spending level is so high that when he eventually got to Amazon, his first purchase was several hundred dollars' worth of books. He recently said to me, "I get on and, click, click, click. I don't even know how much I'm spending there."

High spending power can make a pessimist appear to be an optimist. Yet these two groups have radically different approaches to the Internet. High-income optimists are willing to overcome the difficulty of learning new skills, but high-income pessimists stick with what they already know.

The move to on-line shopping is a bit like a steeplechase—consumers have to clear a lot of technology hurdles. High-income optimists run at breakneck speed and sail over hurdle after hurdle in their quest to master technology. The high-income pessimists, on the other hand, balk at the first fence. If someone comes out on the course and lowers the hurdle—that is, makes the technology easier to use—then the reluctant racers back up and try again. Once the technology hurdles get low enough, the high-income pessimists will race along just as quickly as the high-income optimists.

High-income pessimists buy a lot of well-known and easy-to-use technology but avoid innovations that require effort to learn. For example, high-income pessimists buy cell phones, cordless phones, and home security systems almost as often as affluent optimists do, but they fall way behind high-income optimists on PC ownership, Internet usage, and on-line shopping.

It is not unusual for a high-income pessimist to become comfortable with just one or two technologies. In my father's case, his personal interest in books is so strong that, with time and some help from his friends, he has cleared all the hurdles between him and Amazon. But don't look for a Palm Pilot or a digital phone in his pocket—buying books on-line has not turned him into a technology optimist. He may be one of Amazon's top shoppers, but my father still won't use an answering machine.

Among low-income consumers, pessimists not only balk at technology but also find it prohibitively expensive. Low-income optimists, on the other hand, will do anything in their power to overcome the fact that they are short of money for technology. Low-income optimists seek out PCs and Internet connections at school and in public libraries far more often than other consumers do.

The bottom line is that income by itself does not change a person's attitude toward technology; it just makes a computer more

	Characteristics	Disposable personal income[1]	Cell phone	Penetration		
				PC	On-line[2]	Shop on-line[3]
High-income optimists	Leading technology adopters	$2,979	65%	73%	60%	19%
Low-income optimists	When technology prices drop, they buy	$364	35%	44%	31%	8%
High-income pessimists	Embrace mostly intuitive technologies	$2,437	57%	52%	30%	6%
Low-income pessimists	Technology adoption laggards	$445	25%	22%	10%	2%

1. In billions
2. *On-line* is at least once a month
3. *Shop on-line* is at least once in the past three months.

Source: Forrester Research, Inc.

Figure 5 Consumer Technographic Income Distribution and Technology Penetration

affordable. That is why so many high-income pessimists own a PC but rarely use it. It also explains why so many low-income optimists who don't own PCs find a way to get on-line.

WHAT MOTIVATES CONSUMERS TO USE THE INTERNET

While consumers' technology attitude and income level determine how fast they go on-line, those two factors leave out a most basic question: *Why* do they go on-line? It's not enough to be optimistic about technology and to be able to afford it. A consumer needs a motive.

13

People go on the Internet for many different reasons. One person may seek help for a life-threatening disease, while another keeps up with high school sports scores in their hometown. In fact, when Forrester did open-ended interviews for Technographics, consumers described an amazing array of highly specific reasons for going on-line. In some recent interviews, for example, one person told us that he collected old tin soldiers and went on-line to locate other collectors. Another, an engineer at Dow, went on-line each evening to learn about new research in household chemicals. A third was running her local senior center social calendar on-line.

To make this information useful to business planners, who need to understand at the most basic level what is driving people to go on-line, Forrester decided to classify these myriad motivations. We began by researching human needs, such as the need for food, shelter, love, and approval. Building on work done by the American Psychological Association, Forrester grouped a wide range of needs as they relate to technology. In the end, three groups capture consumers' main motives for going on-line:

- **Career.** Some people are interested primarily in advancing themselves. They seek achievement, recognition, and power over others. Career-motivated optimists see technology as a means to those ends. They use the Internet to stay current with developments in their field of interest, to gain an edge in their business, and to establish themselves as leaders.

- **Family**. Family-motivated consumers use the Internet principally to connect with other people. The desire to nurture family and children and the need of humans to affiliate with one another in social groups underlie the behavior of these consumers. While having children often causes people to become family motivated, it is important to remember that single people can also be family motivated if what they seek on-line is community affiliation.

- **Entertainment.** People's needs for fun, social status, and excitement fall into the category of entertainment. People motivated by entertainment needs see the Internet as a way to get more out of life. They use the Internet for fun—to buy event tickets, play games, and keep up with popular culture. The fast-paced, high-stakes game of day trading appeals mainly to entertainment-oriented consumers.

Naturally, consumers' needs span the entire spectrum. People always have a mix of career, family, and entertainment interests. Yet for each consumer, one of these interest groups dominates the other two, constituting the *primary motivation* for going on-line.

Unlike attitudes toward technology, however, motivations can change quickly—most abruptly around major life events. Becoming a father or experiencing the grave illness of a close friend can thrust

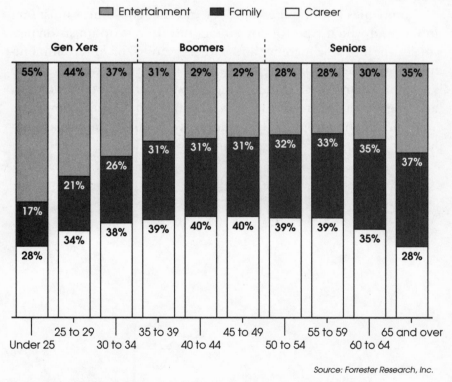

Source: Forrester Research, Inc.

Figure 6 The Technology Optimist's Motivation Life Cycle

a man from being an entertainment-driven Internet frolicker to a family-oriented member of an on-line community. Retirement often shifts a person's focus from career to family, as keeping in touch with children and grandchildren becomes a priority. A promotion or a divorce can bring career needs to the fore. In general, young adults tend to be entertainment oriented, while middle-aged adults focus on career needs, and older adults are more concerned with family issues (see Figure 6).

The most effective way to reach an Internet consumer is to tap into whichever set of needs is foremost in the consumer's mind right now. In other words, motivations are the Internet marketer's main concern. To win consumers, companies must formulate products, services, and messages that respond to people's primary motivations.

Companies fighting the battle for Internet consumers must first understand which types of consumers they have—optimists or pessimists, high or low income, and career-, family-, or entertainment-motivated. Determining the actual makeup of your consumer base is a significant research undertaking. However, in chapter 2, you can take a self-assessment test that will let you estimate your company's consumer Technographics. In addition, we'll look at the actual composition of consumers for two example companies.

CHAPTER 2

Using Technographics to Target Internet Consumers

Consumer Technographics can help new companies identify their best early prospects on the Internet and can tell traditional companies how fast their consumers will go on-line and why. But first they need to figure out what type of consumers they have now—optimists or pessimists? Without this information, it is nearly impossible for a traditional company to know when and how to move its business to the Internet.

Some companies understand their consumers' Technographics instinctively. For example, I know of a woman who has a very successful business selling high-end stationery in an affluent Boston suburb. Her customers are primarily "society women" in their fifties and sixties who have never worked in an office setting. These customers visit her lovely store two or three times a year and spend several hours chatting and selecting personal stationery; it's as much a social event as a commercial one. To introduce any kind of technology into this transaction would backfire, for these consumers regard computers and the Internet with a mixture of curiosity and fear. Ask this entrepreneur about moving her business on-line and she will correctly tell you, "My customers will never go there." She serves *Traditionalists*—high-income, family-motivated technology pessimists—and she knows it.

By contrast, 3Com, maker of the Palm Pilot, surely knows that people who spend $300 or more for the handheld calendar and address book are not only technology savvy but also enjoy the status of

17

owning "cool" new electronic gadgets. You can see them in airport lounges comparing the latest features and discussing just how soon the next version will be available. 3Com executives may not call their customers *Fast Forwards,* but they know that high-income, career-motivated technology optimists are the ones keeping them in business.

Yet for most companies, figuring out whether existing customers are going to be Internet enthusiasts or not is more difficult than it looks. After all, a company that has been selling soap or cars or home mortgages has never had to think about whether these same consumers possess the attitudes toward technology that will make them eager to buy a PC, go on-line, and shop there.

Take, as an example, the European company Prémaman, which sells expensive, elegant clothing for children. Prémaman has established a following throughout Europe among wealthy parents who want their children to be well turned out. An initial foray into the U.S. market has gone very well, with successful stores opening in Miami, Chicago, and New York. I recently met the president of this company and asked him whether he intended to open an Internet store. "I believe we will," he said. "But, I am not sure how popular the Internet shopping will be for our customers," he said. "Our customers like to see the clothing and touch it before they buy."

No doubt this has been true in the past. However, Technographics research suggests that, at least in the United States, Prémaman's customers could behave very differently in the future. Who buys expensive children's clothing? Mainly, it's well-educated, high-income women with children. A quick cut at the Technographics data for this segment reveals that Prémaman target customers in the United States are very optimistic about technology. Fifty-two percent of the women between the ages of twenty-four and thirty-nine who have both a high income and children are technology optimists. The mothers employed in white-collar jobs are the most technology savvy of all— an important fact for Prémaman, since at-work mothers have more money and less time for shopping than those at home do. Technographics suggests that Prémaman would benefit enormously from establishing an Internet store for the U.S. market, perhaps one specifically targeted at very high income working mothers.

The best way to figure out the Technographic composition of your company's target consumer base is to interview consumers directly. However, doing field research with consumers isn't always practical. One way Forrester helps clients avoid the survey step is to segment an existing customer database into thirty or more very specific demographic categories. By creating a weighted average of the technology attitudes usually found in these demographic groups, we can estimate what percent of a company's customers are probably technology optimists.

However, even this method requires a lot of statistical work. For this book, I wanted to create a back-of-the-envelope test so quick and easy that you could figure out what kind of consumers your company serves right now. This test cannot offer a 100 percent accurate measure of consumer technology optimism. But, as we will see, it gives a useful estimate of how quickly a company's consumers will move on-line.

INTERPRETING THE RESULTS OF THE QUICK TEST FOR TECHNOGRAPHICS

The quick test will put a company's consumer base into one of three categories (see Figure 1):

- **Early Adopters**. The first consumers to get on-line and shop are high-income technology optimists—people who embrace technology and earn enough to afford PCs and Internet connections. Companies like Prémaman, whose consumers are mostly early adopters, can conclude that up to a quarter of their consumers were already shopping on-line by the end of 1999 and that almost all of them will be by the end of 2003.

- **Mainstream**. A midrange score on the quick test indicates that a company's customers are divided evenly between optimists and pessimists and between high- and low-income consumers. Mainstream consumers will be as much as two years slower than early adopters in moving to on-line shopping. Consumers in the mainstream category move more slowly either because they are

			Points
1) Are your target consumers men or women?		More than 70%	3
(The North American average is 49% male)	Percent	40% to 70%	2
	male:	10% to 39%	1
		Under 10%	0

			Points
2) How well educated are your consumers?		More than 60%	3
(The North American average is 47% with	Percent with	50% to 59%	2
some college)	some college:	40% to 49%	1
		Under 40%	0

			Points
3) What is their median household income?	Median	More than $70	3
(The North American average is $36	household	$45 to $69	2
thousand)	income:	$25 to $44	1
	(thousands)	Under $25	0

			Points
4) Do your target customers have any		More than 50%	3
children at home? *(The North American*	Percent with	40% to 49%	2
average is 34% with children)	children under	30% to 39%	1
	18:	Under 30%	0

			Points
5) What is the median age of your customers?		Under 25	3
(The North American average is 45 years old)	Median age:	25 to 39	2
		40 to 55	1
		More than 56	0

If your total score was:	Your target customers are:	
11 to 15	**Early adopters**	
6 to 10	**Mainstream**	
0 to 5	**Laggards**	

Source: Forrester Research, Inc.

Figure 1   The Quick Test for Technographics

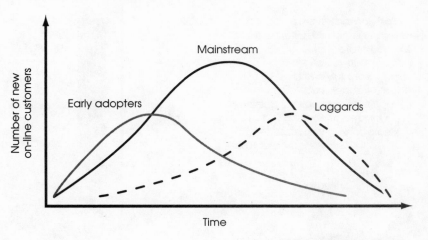

Source: Forrester Research, Inc.

Figure 2 A Technographics View of New Consumer Internet Adoption

pessimists about technology or because they have low income—but not both. People who face both obstacles are laggards.

- **Laggards**. Last to move on-line will be low-income technology pessimists. These' consumers lack the interest and the resources to become on-line shoppers. In fact, many of them may *never* go on-line.

In reality, every company's consumer base has a mix of early, mainstream, and laggard consumers. What the quick test indicates is where a company should center its strategy with regard to the Internet (see Figure 2).

Let's take a look at how this works for a company whose consumers are largely *early adopters*—Starbucks Coffee. Starbucks's score of eleven on the quick test reflects the fact that its consumers are well-educated, high-income people who are slightly younger than the national average. From this result, Starbucks can conclude that a heavy percentage of its consumers will be among the earliest Internet adopters.

A look at the actual, measured Technographics profile for Starbucks confirms the main conclusion of the quick test and offers further insight (see Figure 3).

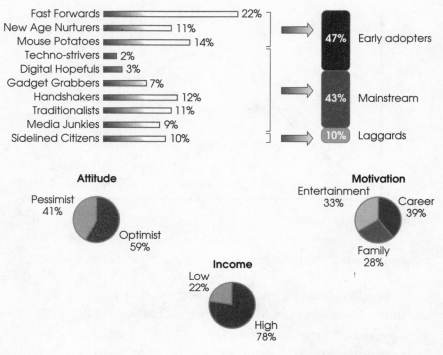

Source: 1998 Fall Mediamark Research, Inc.

Figure 3 Technographics of Starbucks Consumers

Starbucks's Technographics leans heavily toward *high-income optimists* and favors *career-motivated* consumers. Still, a significant group of Starbucks consumers are also high-income pessimists.

Starbucks's Technographics profile indicates that the company should focus its on-line offerings around the needs of people who use the Internet for self-advancement. Moreover, the company must balance the needs of the majority optimists against a significant minority of pessimists. Optimists, particularly career-oriented ones, expect Starbucks to be an on-line leader. Yet the pessimist mainstreamers who go to Starbucks to hang out in the deep purple chairs and read the latest selections from Oprah's book club will need guidance and reassurance if they are to patronize Starbucks on-line as well.

Finally, it would worry me if I ran Starbucks to see how really *unpopular* the company is with low-income technology optimists. This result is not surprising, since Starbucks sells a very expensive product in its category. Yet it does indicate that Starbucks is pricing its coffee outside the reach of many on-line consumers, particularly the college students and recent graduates who make up a large part of the low-income optimist segment.

Now let's look at a similar product whose consumer base is mostly *mainstream*—Maxwell House coffee. Maxwell House scores an eight on the quick test, reflecting this brand's somewhat older and more moderate-income consumers. This back-of-the-envelope calculation is once again confirmed by the actual Technographics profile of Maxwell House (see Figure 4).

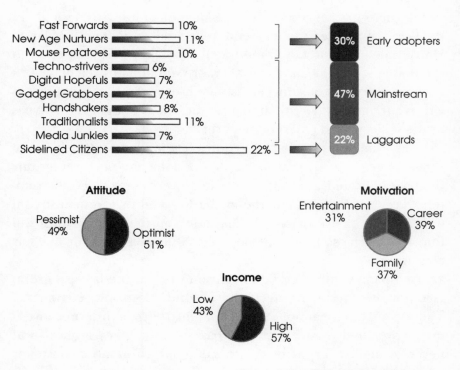

Source: 1998 Fall Mediamark Research, Inc.

Figure 4   Technographics of Maxwell House Consumers

Fifty-one percent of Maxwell House's consumers are technology optimists, which nearly reflects the population average. In fact, this Technographics pattern is typical for any mass consumer brand that holds a large share of its market. Wal-Mart's Technographics, for example, fall within a percentage point or two of Maxwell House's numbers in all ten Technographic categories.

Maxwell House and other mass brands face a significant challenge vis-à-vis competitors such as Starbucks that serve more early adopters. Starbucks's Internet mission is clear—become an on-line leader selling high-end coffee. But Maxwell House must consider the needs of a heavily mainstream consumer base that balances low-income optimists and high-income pessimists. Not only that, Maxwell House must respond to the early adopters and laggards at either end of the Technographics spectrum because together these extremes add up to half the brand's consumers.

For mass-market companies like Maxwell House, strength lies in the fact that their consumers tend to be family oriented. If Maxwell House can appeal to family-motivated early adopters on-line, it can use that base as a means to attract more timid mainstreamers. As a rule, mainstream consumers trust family-oriented early adopters as a reference group more than they do the power-hungry career types or the self-centered entertainment seekers.

Few companies that take the quick test will land squarely in the *laggard* category. For that to happen, a company must serve only the least-educated, poorest people in the economy. Even discounters like Payless Shoes emerge at the low end of the mainstream with a score of five or six. Yet all large consumer companies will find that laggards represent between 20 and 25 percent of their consumers.

Companies with such significant interests in the laggard group face tough investment decisions around electronic commerce. These companies cannot expect to amortize their Internet investments over their entire customer base because many laggards will never go on-line. Laggards create a drag effect on large consumer companies—one they must consciously overcome in order to win the battle for mainstream consumers.

In the next three chapters, we'll look more closely at the different consumer Technographics groups and consider strategic trade-offs inherent in serving each one. The battle for Internet consumers begins with early adopters, and that is where we'll begin. Start-ups have made their inroads in this area, and traditional companies must fight back fast to get in the game. After that, we'll look at how Internet competition will shift as more and more mainstream consumers begin to shop on-line. Finally, we'll look at strategies for managing the laggards in every traditional company's consumer base.

CHAPTER 3

Reaching Early Adopters

The battle for Internet consumers begins with the early adopters—high-income technology optimists. As a group, these sixty million consumers wield enormous influence over the fate of both Internet start-ups and traditional companies. Start-ups must attract early adopters in order to survive, while slower-moving traditional companies risk losing these well-to-do, technology-savvy consumers. In this chapter we'll see exactly who these people are and what companies must do to win their business.

Early adopters are the most Internet-connected of all consumers. As of the beginning of 1999, 60 percent were already on-line—and another 20 percent planned to go on-line by the end of the year. Yet being connected is only part of the story. Early adopters control nearly $3 trillion in spending power—money they can shift from traditional retail channels to Internet storefronts. Will they? Technographics research indicates that the answer is yes—for three reasons.

First, nearly all early adopters say they expect to shop on-line, and the time lag between when they first go on-line and when they begin to shop is shrinking. In 1997, the only consumers who shopped on-line were those with three or four years of Internet experience. Newer on-line consumers sometimes visited Web stores, but they rarely purchased anything. By 1999, this time lag collapsed to just eighteen months.

Second, early adopters who *do* shop on-line earn so much that once they become comfortable shopping in a new way, their spending increases rapidly. Early adopters spend twice as much on average in their second year as they did in their first.

Third, the main obstacle for on-line early adopters who *didn't* shop in 1999 was fear of credit-card fraud. In all likelihood, this objection will be steadily erased as time passes and consumers gain experience. Internet credit-card fraud actually occurs at a far lower rate than does telephone fraud. Besides, credit-card companies already protect consumers from *any* loss over $50 resulting from stolen cards.

The conclusion is easy to draw. By 2003, over three-quarters of high-income technology optimists will be on-line shoppers. In total, these consumers represent a $70 billion to $80 billion market opportunity for Internet businesses.

Businesses that want to reach early adopters can count on them being on the Internet. Early adopters already have the optimistic attitudes required to master new technology, and they have enough income to buy a PC and go on-line. But to get them to buy on-line, marketers must tap early adopters' primary motives for going on the Internet—self-advancement, affiliation with other people, or enjoyment. We can divide early adopters by their motivations into three groups:

- *Fast Forwards*—high-income optimists motivated by career needs.
- *New Age Nurturers*—high-income optimists motivated by family needs.
- *Mouse Potatoes*—high-income optimists motivated by entertainment needs.

FAST FORWARDS: WINNING CAREER-MINDED EARLY ADOPTERS

The earliest of the early adopters are *Fast Forwards*—a group so easy to distinguish from other types of consumers that they are almost a caricature. Imagine a married couple, both with briefcases, bidding each other good-bye before work at 7:00 A.M. on a city street corner. As they part, the woman gets out her cellular phone to confirm her afternoon appointment across town, and the man responds to a vibrating pager on his belt that gives him a message from his accountant and a stock price update. Taking out his handheld computer, the husband notes down a to-do for their tax returns and records the new stock values. Meanwhile, the wife accesses their home voice-mail remotely and learns that the kids' summer-camp schedule has changed. So she phones the second line at their house to leave a message for the nanny that she'll fax home the revised schedule as soon as she can download it from the Internet to her computer at work.

This urban couple belongs to the elite of technology consumers, whom we estimate to include twenty-four million adults. Their deeply rooted belief that technology can improve their lives is evident in their consumption patterns: Seventy-seven percent of Fast Forwards have a PC in their home, compared to just 48 percent of the general population. In fact, Fast Forwards are far more likely than most people to have every other kind of digital technology as well, including cell phones, pagers, second phone lines, and in-home fax machines (see Figure 1).

Fast Forwards are nearly twice as likely as other consumers to use a palm computer or pay their bills over the Internet.

Fast Forwards not only possess more digital equipment than the rest of us; they are willing to use it. By early 1999, over 60 percent of Fast Forwards used their computers almost every single day and could be described as regular on-line users—and 20 percent more thought they would by the end of the year. One reason for this heavy computer use is that most Fast Forwards are white-collar workers. In fact, over a fifth of them operate a business out of their home.

Not surprisingly, Fast Forwards are both educated and affluent. Their median annual income is $71,000, nearly twice that of the overall population, and 21 percent of Fast Forwards earn over $100,000 per year. Fast Forwards are the best-educated group of consumers in America. Half of them live in households supported by a dual-income couple.

Every on-line business must consider the needs of Fast Forwards, since they are among the leading on-line buyers of every

	Fast Forwards	Overall Population
Demographics		
Male	**68%**	49%
Under 30	**11%**	14%
30 to 44	**44%**	35%
45 and over	**45%**	51%
Median age	**44**	45
Married	**70%**	54%
At least some college	**76%**	47%
Median income	**$71,000**	$36,000
Children under 18	**44%**	34%
Technology Habits		
Have additional phone line	**40%**	25%
Have fax machine	**36%**	21%
Have pager	**41%**	29%
Have a cellular phone	**68%**	46%
Have a palm computer	**10%**	6%
Own a PC	**77%**	48%
Use a computer at work	**82%**	47%
On-line Activities		
Go on-line regularly	**62%**	33%
Purchase on-line	**20%**	9%
Do financial transactions on-line	**7%**	2%

Source: Forrester Research, Inc.

Figure 1   A Technographics Profile of Fast Forwards

type of product in these early days of the Internet. But Fast Forwards are especially important to industries such as travel, financial services, home office equipment, and computer- or communications-related gear because their career interests put them at the very center of the target customer base (see Figure 2).

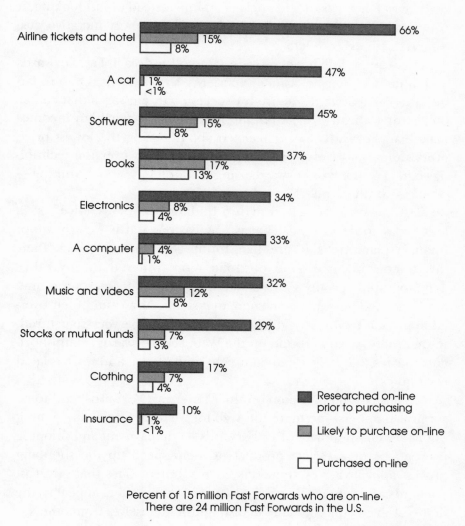

Airline tickets and hotel — 66% / 15% / 8%
A car — 47% / 1% / <1%
Software — 45% / 15% / 8%
Books — 37% / 17% / 13%
Electronics — 34% / 8% / 4%
A computer — 33% / 4% / 1%
Music and videos — 32% / 12% / 8%
Stocks or mutual funds — 29% / 7% / 3%
Clothing — 17% / 7% / 4%
Insurance — 10% / 1% / <1%

■ Researched on-line prior to purchasing

▨ Likely to purchase on-line

☐ Purchased on-line

Percent of 15 million Fast Forwards who are on-line.
There are 24 million Fast Forwards in the U.S.

Source: Forrester Research, Inc.

Figure 2   Products Fast Forwards Research and Purchase On-line

Take travel, for example. Among Fast Forwards that go on-line regularly, 66 percent say they usually research travel plans on-line. Yet by early 1999, only 8 percent of these same Fast Forwards had ever actually bought a travel ticket or booked a hotel reservation on-line. Consumers didn't buy tickets because they worried that their credit card would be stolen. If an on-line travel competitor can persuade Fast Forwards to book tickets on-line instead of just looking, it could steal away the traditional travel agents' most lucrative customers: business travelers.

How can on-line travel providers and others reach Fast Forwards and influence their behavior? Experience shows that it is best to tap into the Fast Forwards' desire for success with messages that center on "getting ahead" or "getting an advantage." Their high incomes make Fast Forwards less concerned about getting the lowest price every time—and convenience alone will not win over the technology elite. For the Fast Forward, using technology is about winning—on the job and in life.

Fast Forwards are interested in finding "the best choice" or "a better way to do things." That is why Fast Forwards eagerly adopt financial-planning software like Intuit Quicken and track their investments in an on-line portfolio more often than any other Technographic group. Fast Forwards are willing to spend the time to set up such personal management systems. As a result, their overall approach to the World Wide Web tends to be very structured. Rather than wander around on the Web, Fast Forwards set up shortcuts to sites that help them complete both home- and work-related tasks quickly.

Because of the premium on their time, Fast Forwards tend to be surgical shoppers—going to the Web for what they need and getting out fast. Web sites that let Fast Forwards set up payment and shipping instructions or preselect products to help speed up the shopping process appeal to these time-starved consumers. Sites that give Fast Forwards access to exclusive products or limited offers appeal to the desire of the technology elite to distinguish themselves from others.

One site that has appealed very well to Fast Forwards is aa.com—American Airlines' frequent traveler club. While visitors have access to many of the site's features, members can log on to gain access to their frequent-flier accounts, special fares and travel packages, and flight bookings. AA.com wins with Fast Forwards because they can do business with American on their schedule. It is faster and easier to get flight information on aa.com than to call American's voice-activated phone system—in short, it's "a better way."

AA.com has clearly met the needs of Fast Forwards. In the year that followed the site's relaunch in June 1998, nearly half of American's top-tier frequent fliers logged on to aa.com, and these consumers averaged five visits a month. The site's monthly revenue increased fivefold from June 1998 to June 1999, and aa.com is on track to sell $500 million in 1999.[1]

It is easy for American Airlines to reach its Fast Forward targets; it already has their AAdvantage information and includes the airline's Web site address on its regular home mailings for the frequent flier program. Partly as a result of this existing database asset, American attracted more than two million customers to aa.com in the first year. But how can other companies reach the Fast Forward technology elite?

Once again, career motivation provides a key. Fast Forwards flock to any means at their disposal to get ahead in their life endeavors. When they are off-line, Fast Forwards read more business magazines, financial newspapers, and technology-related publications than any other group.[2] *The Economist, The Wall Street Journal, Business Week,* and *The Industry Standard* all address Fast Forward audiences.

Advertising on television has a more limited appeal. While it is possible to reach a high percentage of Fast Forwards by running Super Bowl ads—as several barely solvent dotcom businesses have done—the evidence suggests that, on the whole, television offers a hit-or-miss proposition. Fast Forwards spend less time watching TV than most consumers do; these earliest adopters represent just 10 percent of the overall audience during prime time.[3] That makes television a very costly way to reach Fast Forwards.

In fact, Fast Forwards are easier to reach on-line, where they constitute nearly a quarter of the population (see Figure 3).

Percent of total Fast Forwards who:

Watch any weekly television show	79%	62%	Go on-line once a week
Watch the Super Bowl	45%	47%	Visit search sites
		34%	Visit company or product sites
Watch the Academy Awards	23%	20%	Visit news sites
Watch *60 Minutes*	18%	14%	Visit sports sites
Watch *Oprah Winfrey*	7%	8%	Visit entertainment sites
Percent of TV viewers which are Fast Forwards	10%	23%	Percent of on-line users which are Fast Forwards
Television			**On-line**

Source: Forrester Research, Inc.
and 1998 Fall Mediamark Research Inc.

Figure 3   Reaching Fast Forwards via Television and On-line

Fast Forwards can be found at the Web sites of the *New York Times* and *Business Week*. But companies that want to reach Fast Forwards on-line must look beyond traditional media venues. Fast Forwards frequent search sites like Yahoo! and Excite, where they often set up personal pages. From these search sites, Fast Forwards go directly to the Web sites of companies whose products they want to research or buy. Therefore, the best way to reach Fast Forwards on the Web is to advertise on the search sites and on the Web sites of noncompetitors that serve the same group. For example, American Airlines could advertise on the Hertz site, and vice versa.

In sum, Fast Forwards represent the best first opportunity for electronic commerce sites—especially in the areas of travel, financial services, and new communications or computer equipment. Because of their aggressive adoption of any technology that helps them to get ahead in their life endeavors, Fast Forwards will be among the first buyers of every type of product on-line. Companies that want to reach this group must leverage their career focus to locate Fast Forwards and craft a message that will appeal to their sense of personal achievement. The desire for distinction separates Fast Forwards from other early adopters.

NEW AGE NURTURERS: GIVING FAMILIES WHAT THEY WANT ON-LINE

The Fast Forwards are so distinctive in their technology-driven lifestyle that it is easy to overlook a huge, and in some ways more powerful, class of consumers: *New Age Nurturers.* These sixteen million family-oriented people also have high incomes and technology optimism, but their motivation to use technology is entirely different. New Age Nurturers are less concerned with personal achievement and recognition than Fast Forwards are. Instead, New Age Nurturers center their lives and their consumption patterns on personal affiliations.

The preference for family and community shows up in the demographics of New Age Nurturers: 84 percent live in family households—that is, homes with two or more members who are related to one another. There are more females among New Age Nurturers than among any other early adopter group (see Figure 4).

New Age Nurturers form the affluent center of the baby-boom generation. Like Fast Forwards, New Age Nurturers tend to live near cities, but many have opted for homes in suburbs as they raise their children.

For companies that want to establish leadership in electronic commerce, New Age Nurturers are in some ways the most critical consumer group to win over. Even though Fast Forwards will be quicker to adopt Internet shopping, New Age Nurturers will not be far behind—and they are much more credible opinion leaders for the mainstream. From the surge in the popularity of sport utility vehicles to the rising demand for all-cotton clothing, fresher food at the supermarket, second mortgages, and baby joggers, the New Age

	New Age Nurturers	Overall Population
Demographics		
Male	54%	49%
Under 30	9%	14%
30 to 44	41%	35%
45 and over	50%	51%
Median age	45	45
Married	75%	54%
At least some college	67%	47%
Median income	$62,000	$36,000
Children under 18	45%	34%
Technology Habits		
Have additional phone line	35%	25%
Have fax machine	28%	21%
Have pager	35%	29%
Have a cellular phone	62%	46%
Have a palm computer	7%	6%
Own a PC	74%	48%
Use a computer at work	68%	47%
On-line Activities		
Go on-line regularly	56%	33%
Purchase on-line	17%	9%
Do financial transactions on-line	5%	2%

Source: Forrester Research, Inc.

Figure 4 A Technographics Profile of New Age Nurturers

Nurturers visibly lead other consumers. Very simply, the tastes of New Age Nurturers set trends.

For traditional companies, doing business on the Internet with New Age Nurturers ought to be easy. New Age Nurturers prefer to buy their favorite brands, but they would like to buy these brands at the best price possible. When family-oriented consumers go on-line, they want to buy products they like from retailers they know. The question is, can they? Many of the companies that these consumers normally patronize have such poorly constructed Web sites that after a couple of tries, family-oriented consumers decide to go elsewhere (see Figure 5).

I recently had the kind of frustrating experience that many New Age Nurturers encounter on the Internet. I normally do a lot of business with The Pleasant Company, a subsidiary of Mattel, which makes the "American Girl" dolls for girls ages eight to twelve. When my daughter's birthday neared, I didn't have a Pleasant Company catalog on hand. So I decided to visit the company's Web site to see what new toys were offered.

On the Internet, my main hurdle was finding the company on-line at all. When I entered "American Girl Dolls" on my favorite search site, I was horrified to get back a listing of overtly pornographic sites. Not only that, but the advanced technology on the site matched my search request with "context sensitive" banner advertising that featured tongue-thrusting, double-D cup models in their underwear. I don't consider myself a prude, but frankly, seeing those images when I was focused on buying a doll for my second-grade daughter made me uneasy. When I finally did get to the Pleasant Company site, I found that they didn't even sell the dolls on-line yet. After this experience, I won't go to American Girls on-line myself; and I won't let my daughter go either, for fear of what she'll see on the way.

Likewise, my effort to help my friend buy a Graco Duo stroller from Toys "R" Us turned out badly. We got to Toys "R" Us all right, but despite the fact that we knew both the brand and the specific product we wanted, Toys "R" Us on-line just couldn't show us the stroller. We shopped by department, looked in hot items, and even tried the search feature, but we found no Graco stroller.

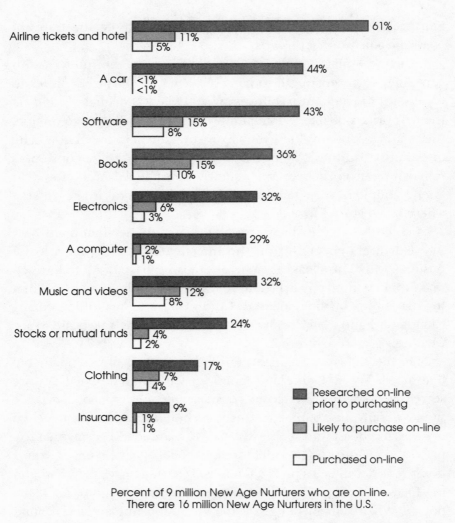

Airline tickets and hotel — 61% / 11% / 5%
A car — 44% / <1% / <1%
Software — 43% / 15% / 8%
Books — 36% / 15% / 10%
Electronics — 32% / 6% / 3%
A computer — 29% / 2% / 1%
Music and videos — 32% / 12% / 8%
Stocks or mutual funds — 24% / 4% / 2%
Clothing — 17% / 7% / 4%
Insurance — 9% / 1% / 1%

■ Researched on-line prior to purchasing
■ Likely to purchase on-line
□ Purchased on-line

Percent of 9 million New Age Nurturers who are on-line.
There are 16 million New Age Nurturers in the U.S.

Source: Forrester Research, Inc.

Figure 5 Products New Age Nurturers Research and Purchase On-line

Finally, I suggested that we go to an on-line community that I belong to called Parent Soup. There we found another on-line store, one I'd never heard of before, called iBaby.com. iBaby had every kind of Graco product, plus a lot of other strollers, too. We found the stroller she wanted, and bang, Toys "R" Us lost us both as Internet consumers.

These experiences demonstrate just how much damage a consumer company can do to its brand when it neglects the needs of family-oriented early adopters. Maybe Toys "R" Us executives didn't believe it was prudent to spend as much money as it would have cost to build a decent Web site in 1999. Perhaps The Pleasant Company just couldn't make its presence on search sites a priority as it expanded its main product line. But I would bet that, when the executives at these companies did the math, none of them took into account how many New Age Nurturers would have a bad experience with their brands in 1999—and how many other people would hear about it.

To win the business of New Age Nurturers, companies must help these consumers fulfill their children's needs and improve their family lives. The same messages about dependability, safety, togetherness, and child rearing that established many consumer brands in the first place remain relevant as New Age Nurturers move online—but only if the brands continue to live up to their names.

The good news for traditional companies is that New Age Nurturers will probably remain loyal customers until a company disappoints them. The danger for traditional companies is that if they fail to build an effective Web presence, New Age Nurturers will either develop unattractive new associations with the brand, as I did with American Girls, or fail to find the brand on the Internet altogether.

To prevent brand erosion, traditional sellers of children's clothing, furniture, food, toys, educational software, books, family cars, appliances, and banking or insurance services must not only have a credible Web presence, but they must also direct their existing customers toward it—through every current communications channel.

Reaching New Age Nurturers is a matter of saturating the venues that attract affluent families. Television advertising is somewhat more effective for New Age Nurturers than for Fast Forwards—especially on newsmagazine shows like *Dateline, 60 Minutes,* and *20/20* and on channels that feature science fiction or children's shows.[4] Print campaigns directed through magazines that target women, teens, children, and parents also touch these consumers' desire for affiliation well.

Traditional companies that want to extend their existing brand relationships with New Age Nurturers should make it as easy as possible for these consumers to find them on the Internet. Therefore, any direct-mail marketing efforts and all product packaging should direct New Age Nurturers to a brand's Web site address. In addition, companies must ensure that their brands are fairly and accurately represented in search results at major Internet search sites such as Yahoo!, Microsoft Network, America Online, and At Home.

MOUSE POTATOES: TAPPING THE SPENDING POWER OF ENTERTAINMENT SEEKERS

Like the Fast Forwards and the New Age Nurturers, *Mouse Potatoes* are both optimistic about technology and financially well off. But Mouse Potatoes use technology for fun. Far more than other early adopters, Mouse Potatoes frequent sports sites, visit adult entertainment venues, look up movie information and reviews, and play on-line games.

Mouse Potatoes form a group of some nineteen million consumers (see Figure 6). Predominantly urban and male, this group's center is five years younger than other early adopters. Mouse Potatoes' median income of $59,000 is slightly lower than that of other early adopter groups, but their money goes much farther because they don't have to feed a family, pay tuition, or hire baby-sitters. For unlike Fast Forwards and New Age Nurturers, many of whom are raising families, the majority of Mouse Potatoes live in one- or two-member households. Three-quarters of them have no children. In short, these consumers have both money and time, and they're out to have fun.

When Mouse Potatoes go on-line, their activity is much different from either the surgical efficiency of the Fast Forwards or the community-seeking behavior of the New Age Nurturers. Mouse Potatoes are like kids at an amusement park. They are maddeningly active, scarcely spending more than a few minutes on any one task. Mouse Potatoes love to watch TV or listen to the radio while they're on-

	Mouse Potatoes	Overall Population
Demographics		
Male	58%	49%
Under 30	22%	14%
30 to 44	41%	35%
45 and over	37%	51%
Median age	40	45
Married	45%	54%
At least some college	74%	47%
Median income	$59,000	$36,000
Children under 18	25%	34%
Technology Habits		
Have additional phone line	36%	25%
Have fax machine	32%	21%
Have pager	39%	29%
Have a cellular phone	65%	46%
Have a palm computer	9%	6%
Own a PC	69%	48%
Use a computer at work	74%	47%
On-line Activities		
Go on-line regularly	59%	33%
Purchase on-line	21%	9%
Do financial transactions on-line	6%	2%

Source: Forrester Research, Inc.

Figure 6   A Technographics Profile of Mouse Potatoes

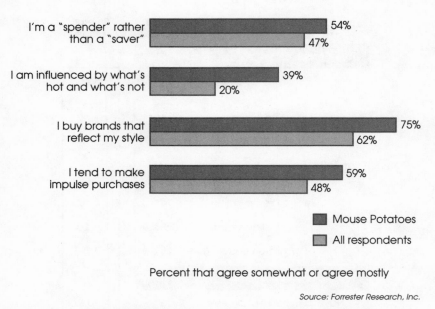

Figure 7   How Mouse Potatoes Differ from Other Consumers

line, and some report that they even read magazines while they wait for Web pages to load.

Because of their high activity level, Mouse Potatoes often buy on impulse—leaving careful price and value comparisons to less affluent or more mindful people (see Figure 7).

Mouse Potatoes like to buy books, music CDs, videos, fashion clothing, consumer electronics, and event tickets on-line. These categories offer plenty of choices and many items that appeal because they're "hot."

Buying the latest music, gadgets, and gear confers a kind of status that Mouse Potatoes seek—but this status has a different quality than the type of status sought by Fast Forwards. While career-minded people are looking to get ahead of others, entertainment types buy the latest new products because they get a kick out of it.

Mouse Potatoes will also buy on-line for convenience—especially mundane items, which they do not want to take the time to shop for in person. So, for instance, more Mouse Potatoes than New Age Nurturers have signed up for on-line grocery services—even though you might predict the opposite. The same holds true for housewares. "Why waste your life thinking about garbage cans and mops? Just click and get it delivered," thinks the Mouse Potato.

But don't expect grocery and housewares shopping by Mouse Potatoes to lead mainstream consumers on-line in the way New Age Nurturers will. Entertainment-oriented consumers are fickle customers. They don't care much about homemaking activities, and their buying is not the result of careful, "what's best for the family" decision making. It is unlikely that Mouse Potatoes will become trendsetters in these categories.

Two other strong on-line shopping categories for Mouse Potatoes are financial services and travel—both areas where impulse behavior can lead to big spending (see Figure 8).

They may not balance their checkbooks, but Mouse Potatoes are the most active consumers of all at the ATM machine—and they are second only to Fast Forwards in on-line investing. Low-cost trading has turned small-lot investing into a new kind of game. In travel, Fast Forwards have been quicker than Mouse Potatoes to buy tickets. But that is changing. Seventeen percent of Mouse Potatoes who are on-line say they will begin buying travel tickets over the Internet during 1999—good news for an industry that needs to sell fewer discounted air tickets and more on-line vacation packages in order to be profitable.

So Mouse Potatoes have money to spend, and they're willing to spend it on-line—if you can get their attention. The question is, how?

To catch a Mouse Potato, start with television. More than any other early adopters, Mouse Potatoes watch TV—sports events, hot evening dramas, and movie channels above all. Mouse Potatoes love their TVs and everything that connects to them: They are leading adopters of VCRs and, more recently, digital video disks. More Mouse Potatoes have big-screen TVs than anybody else does, and these monster tubes are almost universally connected to either cable or satellite.

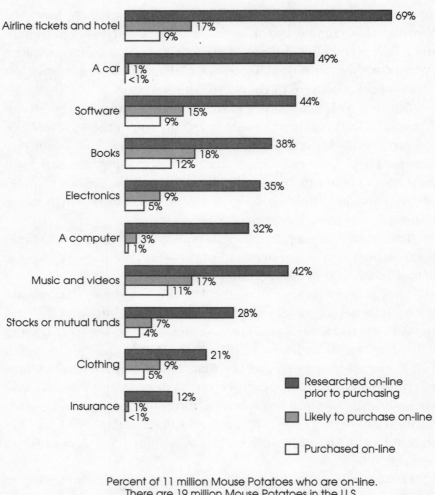

Airline tickets and hotel — 69% / 17% / 9%
A car — 49% / 1% / <1%
Software — 44% / 15% / 9%
Books — 38% / 18% / 12%
Electronics — 35% / 9% / 5%
A computer — 32% / 3% / 1%
Music and videos — 42% / 17% / 11%
Stocks or mutual funds — 28% / 7% / 4%
Clothing — 21% / 9% / 5%
Insurance — 12% / 1% / <1%

■ Researched on-line
   prior to purchasing

■ Likely to purchase on-line

□ Purchased on-line

Percent of 11 million Mouse Potatoes who are on-line.
There are 19 million Mouse Potatoes in the U.S.

Source: Forrester Research, Inc.

Figure 8 Products Mouse Potatoes Research and Purchase On-line

Although less compelling than television, print offers good opportunities to reach Mouse Potatoes as well. Magazines like *Sports Illustrated, Entertainment Weekly, People, Cosmopolitan,* and *Vanity Fair* target the entertainment-motivated consumer directly, while Thursday's leisure supplements in every newspaper from the *LA Times* to the

Chicago Tribune are a must-read for the footloose and child-free week-end planner. Newspaper supplements are particularly good for reaching Mouse Potato women, who by and large are more cultured than their male cyber-spud counterparts, and therefore attend ballet, concerts, and exhibitions more often.

On-line, Mouse Potatoes can be hard to pin down because their surfing activity is so unstructured. That said, Mouse Potatoes can be counted on to seek out frequent updates on any kind of content that changes often, such as market news, stock quotes, sports scores, reviews of recent or upcoming events and movies, and—surprise—the weather. Finally, just as they do for every other type of on-line consumer, search sites offer the most likely venue for reaching Mouse Potatoes as they embark on their on-line adventures.

Messages for Mouse Potatoes must zoom in on what matters to them: "New," "fun," and "exciting" are most effective. Avoiding hassle, drudgery, and boredom comes in second. Mouse Potatoes won't respond to the calls of "solid value," "dependability," and "community" that move the New Age Nurturers to action; nor are they as concerned with self-improvement as Fast Forwards are. Psychologist Sigmund Freud's schema offers an easy way to remember the differences among the three. Fast Forwards are ego-driven—"me, me, me" is their mantra. New Age Nurturers are superego types—"us, us, us," they think. Mouse Potatoes are the id of the on-line world—they just want to have fun.

The first twenty-four months of the new millennium offer a critical window of opportunity for companies to establish leadership with the early adopters. During this time, the great majority of early adopters will move from simply being on-line to shopping. Industries that sell predominantly to early adopters—financial services providers, travel agencies, booksellers, music stores, computer makers, and communication suppliers—already are experiencing fundamental changes in their competitive landscapes.

Next to get caught up in the battle for Internet consumers will be companies whose consumers fall more in the mainstream—clothing makers, automobile companies, consumer packaged-goods manufacturers, banks, and the list goes on. For the early adopters will not only bring their own dollars to the Internet but will lead the way for the eighty-eight million consumers of the mainstream. The next chapter describes the path of mainstream consumers toward Internet shopping and outlines how companies can get out ahead of the juggernaut.

CHAPTER 4

The Battle for the Mainstream

Ultimately, mainstream consumers hold the fate of electronic commerce in their hands. Will Internet shopping grow for a few years and then stall out as a $100 billion market—just twice the size of the mail-order catalog business? Or will it grow much larger? The answer depends on the choices made by the eighty-eight million individuals that make up the mainstream. Constituting 43 percent of the population, this group controls 45 percent of the nation's personal spending. Early adopters are first to participate in electronic commerce, but the ultimate prize in this arena is the loyalty of the consumer mainstream.

So much media attention has been focused on the Internet that it seems as if electronic commerce already is a mainstream phenomenon. But in fact, only a minority of the mainstream was on-line in 1999, and very few actually bought anything (see Figure 1).

Even though early adopters have created the initial market opportunity, mainstream consumers must participate if Internet shopping is to become a widespread activity—one that appeals to more than the high-income technology elite.

The battle for the mainstream will be very different from the struggle to attract early adopters. The first consumers on-line incline naturally toward electronic commerce because of their high incomes and optimistic attitudes about technology. Mainstream consumers, on the other hand, face significant obstacles to on-line shopping.

Technographics segments	Number of U.S. adults	Percent on-line	Percent shop on-line	Average annual individual on-line spending
Mainstream	88 million	30%	7%	$700
Techno-strivers Digital Hopefuls Gadget Grabbers	47 million	31%	8%	$680
Handshakers Traditionalists Media Junkies	41 million	30%	6%	$720

Source: Forrester Research, Inc.

Figure 1   Technographics View of Mainstream Consumers

Either they are technology pessimists who don't really want to go on-line or they lack the income to buy a PC and connect to the Internet.

Companies that want to expand their on-line business beyond early adopters must alleviate the fears and budget limitations that keep mainstream consumers from becoming Internet shoppers. The most effective way to understand the mainstream is to divide these consumers into two broad categories: high-income pessimists and low-income optimists.

HIGH-INCOME PESSIMISTS: GETTING THEM TO PARTICIPATE

Figuring out why high-income pessimists don't use their PCs or go on-line more often is one of the toughest challenges of understanding Internet consumers. Even these consumers themselves aren't sure *exactly* what prevents them from being more active on-line. Our research shows that a few high-income pessimists definitely dislike technology, and some fear crashing the computer or making a mistake. However, most high-income pessimists are simply apathetic about the Internet.

This lack of enthusiasm wouldn't matter so much if high-income pessimists didn't control so much spending power. But these forty-one million adults together have $2.4 trillion in disposable income. Without them, the total Internet opportunity is vastly reduced.

Like high-income optimists, pessimists are divided by different primary motivations: *Handshakers* are career-oriented types, focused on getting ahead and distinguishing themselves; *Traditionalists* focus on nurturing their families and community relationships; and *Media Junkies* feed their appetite for fun. But, unlike the optimists, high-income pessimists don't see technology as a way to meet their needs.

Among a group of high-income people, it is tough to identify the pessimists. Demographically, the pessimists look just like the optimists—middle-aged, well-educated, family householders (see Figure 2). High-income pessimists like to drive Jeeps, Volvos, and Toyotas—just like high-income optimists.[1] What's more, high-income consumers share tastes in media. Both like newsmagazine shows and major sporting and entertainment events.[2]

But when it comes to technology, the behavior of high-income pessimists diverges markedly from that of optimists. Although they own a similar number of cellular and cordless phones, both well-known and widely used technologies, high-income pessimists lag behind in Internet usage (see Figure 3).

While 80 percent of the high-income optimists expect to be on-line by the end of 1999, over half the wealthy pessimists say they're not likely to go on-line—maybe not *ever*. This, in spite of that fact that most of these high-income pessimists already own a PC!

The challenge in getting high-income pessimists to shop on-line is that these consumers like to do what they already know how to do. The main issue is *familiarity*. For high-income pessimists, going on the Internet is like taking a trip to the moon: The whole environment is strange. To get comfortable, they need a recognizable landmark—something that makes them feel that everything is going to work out just fine—like a Starbucks coffee shop.

	High-Income Pessimists	Overall Population
Demographics		
Male	**47%**	49%
Under 30	**8%**	14%
30 to 44	**36%**	35%
45 and over	**56%**	51%
Median age	**47**	45
Married	**69%**	54%
At least some college	**56%**	47%
Median income	**$59,000**	$36,000
Children under 18	**38%**	34%
Technology Habits		
Have additional phone line	**27%**	25%
Have fax machine	**21%**	21%
Have pager	**32%**	29%
Have a cellular phone	**57%**	46%
Have a palm computer	**5%**	6%
Own a PC	**52%**	48%
Use a computer at work	**54%**	47%
On-line Activities		
Go on-line regularly	**30%**	33%
Purchase on-line	**6%**	9%
Do financial transactions on-line	**1%**	2%

Source: Forrester Research, Inc.

Figure 2   A Technographics Profile of High-Income Pessimists

	Pessimists	Percent lower	Optimists
Cable TV	76%	3%	78%
Use credit cards	85%	6%	90%
Cordless phone	82%	6%	87%
Cellular phone	57%	14%	65%
Paychecks direct deposited	61%	16%	71%
Own a PC	52%	40%	73%
On-line regularly[1]	30%	100%	60%
Purchase on-line[2]	6%	217%	19%

Increasing complexity of technology

1. At least once a month 2. At least once in the past three months

Source: Forrester Research, Inc.

Figure 3 Comparison of High-Income Consumers' Technology Habits

It's not fun for high-income pessimists to learn to use new technology, but they will if the technology is easy enough and the activity becomes familiar enough. Just 6 percent of high-income pessimists shopped on-line in 1999. For the most part, they bought books (see Figure 4).

It is as if these consumers read about Amazon so much in the newspaper that they finally decided to try out this one site.

The hard part, from the business planner's point of view, is predicting the on-line behavior of high-income pessimists. If Borders had surveyed these consumers just one month before they went to Amazon, they would have said that they wouldn't buy books on-line. Pessimists are, after all, pessimists—they don't think they're going to like using new technology. But sometimes, if a technology is easy enough to use, pessimists are surprised to discover that they were wrong.

51

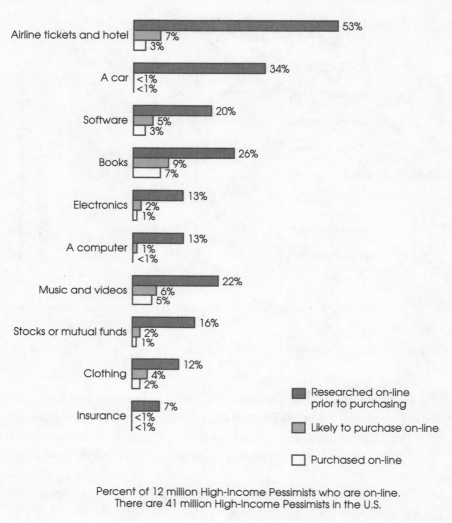

Airline tickets and hotel — 53% / 7% / 3%

A car — 34% / <1% / <1%

Software — 20% / 5% / 3%

Books — 26% / 9% / 7%

Electronics — 13% / 2% / 1%

A computer — 13% / 1% / <1%

Music and videos — 22% / 6% / 5%

Stocks or mutual funds — 16% / 2% / 1%

Clothing — 12% / 4% / 2%

Insurance — 7% / <1% / <1%

■ Researched on-line prior to purchasing

■ Likely to purchase on-line

□ Purchased on-line

Percent of 12 million High-Income Pessimists who are on-line.
There are 41 million High-Income Pessimists in the U.S.

Source: Forrester Research, Inc.

Figure 4 Products High-Income Pessimists Research and Purchase On-line

Fidelity Investments has done a good job of appealing to high-income pessimists as well as optimists. In Forrester's Technographics survey on financial services, consumers ranked Fidelity first among on-line financial-service sites.[3] Top Internet brokerage houses such as Schwab, Datek, and E*TRADE scored highly with early adopters, but Fidelity pleased mainstream consumers more because it offers a sense of familiarity.

Fidelity's consumer Technographics spilt between high-income optimists and pessimists. The company meets the optimists' needs by offering competitive on-line trading rates, the latest tax-free savings plans, and portfolio-tracking services. This has created a following of early adopters within Fidelity's existing consumer base that has helped to generate the positive word of mouth necessary to build confidence among more reticent technology pessimists.

Fidelity then uses consistent branding to make the site feel very familiar. Fidelity presents the same logo, color scheme, and message whether it communicates in print, on TV, or on-line. Peter Lynch, Fidelity's investment guru, appears on the site in the same posture and garb we all recognize from billboard advertisements, magazine spots, and the jackets of his how-to books. Want to plan a sensible asset allocation? Click on Peter Lynch. Looking for tips on how to invest wisely during a turbulent market period? Click on Peter Lynch. The sheer simplicity of knowing and trusting Peter Lynch—and by extension, Fidelity—makes it easier for high-income pessimists to begin their move to on-line investing.

Fidelity also helps coax high-income pessimists along by pouring its development effort into individual and 401(k) retirement account services. High-income pessimists aren't about to become Internet day traders. They want to check on balances, move money around, and maybe buy a few individual stocks. These consumers are funding their children's education and planning for retirement. Fidelity Online helps them meet those goals easily. As a result, the company's Web site went from zero to $200 billion in assets under management in just two years.[4]

The lesson to be learned from Fidelity is that there is tremendous long-term market power in meeting the needs of high-income mainstream consumers for familiarity, brand consistency, and ease of use. Fidelity has been criticized for not making its on-line discount brokerage unit competitive with the likes of AmeriTrade faster. In our investor survey, SureTrade and Datek beat Fidelity in providing high-volume, low-priced Internet brokerage services to aggressive traders. But owning the individual and corporate retirement accounts of high-income pessimists will turn out to be a more profitable and stable business.

LOW-INCOME OPTIMISTS: UNDERSTANDING THE IMPACT OF YOUNG ADULTS

At first glance, low-income optimists appear relatively unimportant for electronic commerce because they wield less than half a trillion dollars in disposable income. But before you dismiss these consumers, look again. Among low-income optimists, 24 percent are under thirty years old. In the general population, only 14 percent of adults are under thirty.

Young people tend to be career-oriented *Techno-Strivers* or fun-loving *Gadget Grabbers* (see Figure 5)—they earn little because they are just starting out. These consumers tend to be single, college-educated, white-collar workers who can expect their incomes to rise as their careers advance and they get married to form dual-income couples (see Figure 6).

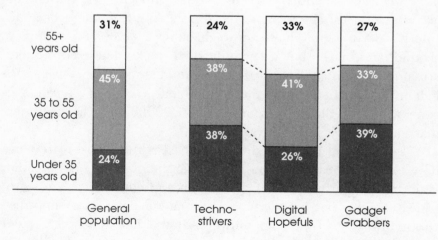

Figure 5 Age Distribution of Low-Income Optimists

	Low-Income Optimists	Low-Income Optimists Under 30	Overall Population
Demographics			
Male	50%	51%	49%
Under 30	24%	100%	14%
30 to 44	34%	0%	35%
45 and over	42%	0%	51%
Median age	41	26	45
Married	41%	41%	54%
At least some college	36%	51%	47%
Median income	$21,000	$23,000	$36,000
Children under 18	34%	40%	34%
Technology Habits			
Have additional phone line	20%	19%	25%
Have fax machine	17%	18%	21%
Have pager	27%	38%	29%
Have a cellular phone	35%	44%	46%
Have a palm computer	6%	6%	6%
Own a PC	44%	58%	48%
Use a computer at work	51%	60%	47%
On-line Activities			
Go on-line regularly	31%	52%	33%
Purchase on-line	8%	15%	9%
Do financial transactions on-line	1%	2%	2%

Source: Forrester Research, Inc.

Figure 6   A Technographics Profile of Low-Income Optimists

Digital Hopefuls, on the other hand, include a very large group of family-oriented retirees who use the Internet to stay in touch with their children and grandchildren.

Demographically, the younger generation differs substantially from older adults. Young optimists are more racially diverse than any other consumer group, with 23 percent minorities, as compared to 17 percent for the population at large. In addition, the optimism gap that exists in the general population between men and women on-line does not appear in young adults. Women between eighteen and thirty-five are just as likely to be technology optimists as men are, and they behave no differently on-line.

Young low-income optimists pursue many activities that other consumers shun. More than any other Technographic group, these consumers love to chat on-line and create personal Web pages. Over a third get their daily news from the Internet—at a time when newspaper readership for this age group is in a long and steady decline. My colleague Shelley Morrisette is fond of saying that, to find out the weather, young adults would rather go on-line than look out the window.

It is difficult, even for technology optimist baby boomers, to fully grasp the impact of computers in the lives of younger adults. Like most consumers, today's young adults began using digital technology personally back in the early 1980s. But while baby boomers were between the ages of twenty-five and thirty-five back then, these younger adults were about ten years old when the first home PCs and cellular telephones appeared.

The generational pattern of younger people being more optimistic about technology appears to accelerate markedly in people under twenty-two. Students now in high school and college use the Internet pervasively, whether or not they own a PC. Once on-line, the majority of people between sixteen and twenty-two chat, exchange instant messages, send electronic cards, download music, and get the news (see Figure 7).

The most interesting part of this finding is that on-line consumers between the ages of sixteen and twenty-two pursue these activities much more frequently than young adults who are just five

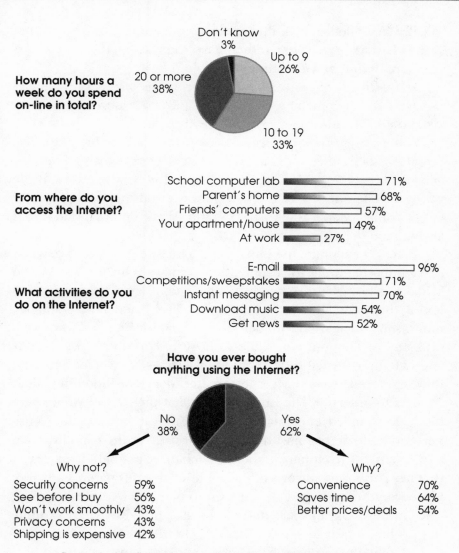

How many hours a week do you spend on-line in total?

Don't know 3%
Up to 9 26%
20 or more 38%
10 to 19 33%

From where do you access the Internet?

School computer lab 71%
Parent's home 68%
Friends' computers 57%
Your apartment/house 49%
At work 27%

What activities do you do on the Internet?

E-mail 96%
Competitions/sweepstakes 71%
Instant messaging 70%
Download music 54%
Get news 52%

Have you ever bought anything using the Internet?

No 38%
Yes 62%

Why not?

Security concerns	59%
See before I buy	56%
Won't work smoothly	43%
Privacy concerns	43%
Shipping is expensive	42%

Why?

Convenience	70%
Saves time	64%
Better prices/deals	54%

Percent of on-line consumers between the ages of 16 and 22.
Eighty-three percent are currently enrolled students.

Source: Forrester Research, Inc.

Figure 7 Activities of 16- to 22-year-olds On-line

to ten years older. In fact, the youngest consumers like the Internet so much that they would rather have high-speed Internet access than a premium movie channel on cable.

As on-line shoppers, low-income optimists spend only half as much as do high-income consumers, and their purchases center around books, music, and software (see Figure 8).

While lower spending levels make young adults less attractive targets for e-commerce than early adopters, clearly it would be dangerous for traditional businesses to ignore the shifting tastes of the younger generation. This is true not only of businesses that usually target young people, such as MTV and Abercrombie & Fitch, but also of staid department stores.

Take, for example, the impact that The Knot, a start-up devoted to wedding planning for young adults, is having on the $45 billion bridal business. Until recently, young people getting married followed the same decades-old formula. The bride-to-be spent six months in anticipation with her mother, planning a hometown wedding and picking out china and silverware. For advice, the mother and daughter turned to traditional magazines like *Brides*. For gifts, they registered at a department store like Macy's or Bloomingdale's.

The founders of The Knot realized that the lives of young people have changed enormously since the traditional wedding business was built. To begin with, the bride usually works—and lives—in a different city from her mother. The chances are better than even that her parents are divorced. Possibly, the groom's parents are, too. Moreover, the bride and groom want to plan the wedding together, since they will pay for part, and maybe all, of the event. This couple has no hometown to speak of, and their friends are so widely dispersed that they will probably plan a "destination" wedding at a vacation resort.

For this couple, planning a wedding begins with creating a Web site. On-line, they will post a schedule of events, directions, and links to the hotels that are holding rooms at a special rate for the guests. To accommodate far-flung friends who cannot come to the actual event, the couple will create an area with photos where well-wishers can exchange messages.

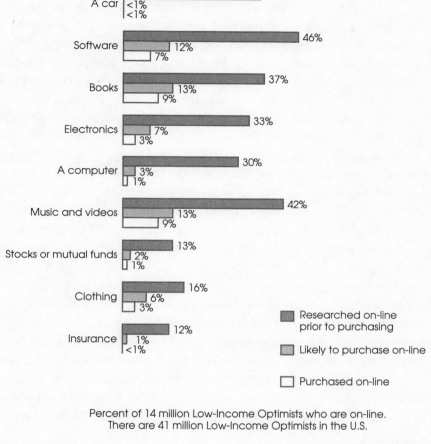

Percent of 14 million Low-Income Optimists who are on-line.
There are 41 million Low-Income Optimists in the U.S.

Source: Forrester Research, Inc.

Figure 8 Products Low-Income Optimists Research and Purchase On-line

The biggest value provided by The Knot and sites like it, however, is managing the gift registry. Registering on-line solves several problems for this couple. First, it lets them select from a wider array of possible gifts. These days, young adults don't limit their choices to china and silver. Instead, they might select camping gear from

L.L. Bean, household goods from Crate & Barrel, or an on-line Fidelity account where guests can make deposits to help them pay for their honeymoon.

Second, anyone who is on the Internet can reach the registry. Among this couple's friends, that means everyone. As far-reaching as the major department stores are, not every guest can get to one.

Third, the on-line system keeps track of what has been purchased—in real time. This is important, since 80 percent of wedding gifts are bought in the three days before the event. Physical store systems just cannot keep up, so 40 percent of what they sell typically has to be exchanged after the wedding.[5]

Finally, the on-line registry lets a couple specify a gift delivery date and location. After all, the last thing the pair wants is for gifts to be delivered to her parent's home before the wedding—which parent? The newlyweds would rather "take delivery" of their gifts at their own home address when they return from their honeymoon.

Because it met the needs of young, low-income optimists, The Knot's revenues grew quickly to over $1 million.[6] The success of The Knot surprised many traditional companies—both magazines and department stores—that held major stakes in the bridal business. But it hasn't taken long for them to respond. Other start-ups, such as DellaJames, WeddingNetwork, and The WeddingChannel, have partnered with major retailers and bridal magazines to compete with The Knot. Even though The Knot originated many new services for engaged couples, the battle for the wedding business—and every other consumer market, for that matter—is far from over.

WINNING MAINSTREAM CONSUMERS

Ultimately, the scope of electronic commerce depends upon getting the second wave of consumers—the mainstream—to buy on-line. Ironically, this imperative puts the start-ups and the traditional companies that are now battling over early adopters on the same team. For it is far from certain that mainstream consumers will become frequent electronic shoppers. Traditional companies need start-ups like The Knot to show them how consumer behavior can change as a result of Internet technology. And start-ups need traditional companies like Fidelity to validate the Internet with reluctant high-income pessimists.

Mainstream consumers do not see a divide between the on-line world and the physical one, the way that many early adopters do. High-income pessimists require consistency between both worlds in order to feel comfortable on-line. Low-income optimists are so accustomed to technology that, for them, the Internet is more a continuation of the physical world than a departure from it. Thus, winning the business of the mainstream requires a multichannel approach that encompasses:

- **Sales.** Mainstream consumers want to buy in person, on the telephone, and by mail—as well as on the Internet. For this to work, a company must have a single electronic system to manage customer accounts across all points of sale. One reason that Fidelity Online is such a comfortable place for mainstream consumers is that their account numbers and names are always the same— whether they communicate with Fidelity on the telephone, by mail, or through the Internet. In the beginning, it is more difficult to be consistent across channels than it is to create a stand-alone Internet business. But the effort pays off, as evidenced by the introduction of bank teller machines. Once mainstream consumers realize they can do business equally well anywhere, they often choose the electronic channel.

- **Service.** To mainstream consumers, The Gap is The Gap, whether it is in the mall or on the Internet. Any artificial separation between the two feels stilted. Young adults expect, for example, to be able to go on-line during their lunch break and put an item in the store on hold until the evening when they can pick it up—why not? For their part, high-income pessimists consider unconnected on-line and off-line business units a confirmation that the technology doesn't work right. Consider how it affects a consumer to place an order on-line and then call to confirm, only to find that the telephone staff doesn't have access to the company's Web site. Connecting on-line and off-line service may be a Herculean task from the IT manager's point of view, but to the consumer, it seems like a basic service.

- **Advertising.** The best way to build a mainstream brand is to advertise on television, where mainstream consumers account for roughly half the audience. But companies that want to avoid the high cost of national advertising can find other ways to insert their brands into consumers' physical world. Gardenescape.com, for example, has brought its brand and its point of sale to the newsstand. As a gardening supplier, this company must appeal to high-income pessimists. So Gardenescape.com created a magazine called *Garden Escape,* where the photography is so beautiful that you might not even notice it's from an Internet-based company. Yet every article includes a shopping list, an 800 number, and the Web site address where consumers can buy the plants and tools they see. Start-ups may not like the prospect of investing in non-Internet marketing channels, but this is what it will take to win mainstream consumers.

When it comes to mainstream consumers, the multichannel imperative favors traditional companies. As hard as it has evidently been for traditional companies to build decent Web sites, it remains far more difficult—and far more expensive—to build a chain of retail stores or train a corps of skilled telephone service representatives. In addition, traditional companies already possess the brands that consumers find familiar, while start-ups must build them from scratch.

However, traditional companies with many mainstream consumers suffer from the inevitable presence of laggards among their customers. Even when they are a minority, laggards pull a company backward toward the old ways of doing business. It's tough to run hard at the Internet opportunity when you know that some of your consumers probably won't ever follow.

What happens, then, to many traditional companies, is that they end up tailoring their Internet strategy to meet the needs of the least likely Internet consumers. If this sounds like a contradiction to you, you're right. This approach is the least desirable of all the alternatives that traditional companies have, yet it is the one they most often pursue. I call this problem the *Laggard Trap*. In the next chapter, we'll examine the causes of the Laggard Trap and identify what steps traditional companies must take to avoid being caught in it.

CHAPTER 5

Avoiding the Laggard Trap

When it comes to joining the on-line competition, the largest consumer companies face a strategic dilemma. These companies serve so many consumers that the Technographic profiles of their businesses looks just like that of the population as a whole. Leaders of these companies can see that Internet usage is a major social and cultural trend, and they believe instinctively that the Internet will affect their business. Yet they serve so many mainstream and laggard consumers that they can't tell how soon or how much the Internet will matter. Thus, they fall into a dilemma: Should they invest heavily in Internet businesses, possibly well in advance of their consumers, or should they wait and risk missing the window of opportunity?

I call this dilemma the *Laggard Trap* because it most often affects companies that serve a high percentage of laggards, or *Sidelined Citizens.* In the Laggard Trap, traditional companies become paralyzed by the preponderance of later adopters in their customer base. These companies either do nothing at all or spend millions of dollars on Internet activities that yield little payoff in consumer business. The companies at greatest risk of falling into the Laggard Trap are those that provide basic necessities. These companies include, almost without exception, the major consumer packaged-goods brands, superstore retailers, auto makers, and banks (see Figure 1).

The problem for these large consumer companies is that many of the normal competitive market signals they watch for seem to be

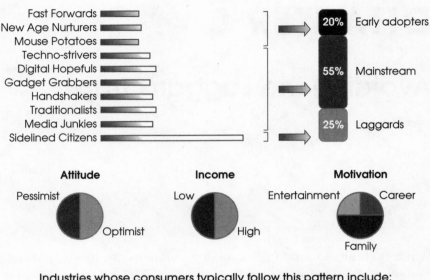

Fast Forwards
New Age Nurturers
Mouse Potatoes
Techno-strivers
Digital Hopefuls
Gadget Grabbers
Handshakers
Traditionalists
Media Junkies
Sidelined Citizens

20% Early adopters

55% Mainstream

25% Laggards

Attitude
Pessimist
Optimist

Income
Low
High

Motivation
Entertainment
Career
Family

Industries whose consumers typically follow this pattern include:

	Examples:
Consumer packaged goods	Procter & Gamble Pillsbury Sara Lee
Large retailers	Wal-Mart Kmart Sears
Automobiles	Ford Chrysler General Motors
Banks	Nations bank BankOne CitiBank

Source: Forrester Research, Inc.

Figure 1   Laggard Trap Technographics

broken when it comes to the Internet. Take, for example, what happened when Unilever, the English soap and packaged-goods conglomerate, announced in July 1998 that it would spend $50 million on Internet advertising over the following three years.

This news was greeted with real enthusiasm by Internet start-ups,

66

which had been struggling to get major advertisers to buy Web banner ads. Before Unilever began spending, most of the advertisements placed on Web sites were from other Web sites. Yahoo!, Microsoft, and America Online were the top sellers of Internet ads—and they were also the leading buyers! More than a third of the so-called "revenues" in Internet advertising were really just circular exchanges among the top few companies. So the Internet companies were thrilled when a real advertiser showed up at the party.

But the same week that Unilever made its announcement, I got a call from the head of one of the world's largest advertising agencies—a company that bills over $5 billion annually. The managing director asked, "What in the world is Unilever doing?" He could find no evidence that Unilever's target consumers could be reached on the Internet, and Forrester's research had clearly indicated that the Internet performs poorly as a branding medium. This executive wanted to know if he had missed something. Had Unilever figured out some angle on the Internet that he and his clients had overlooked? Was Unilever going to sell laundry detergent and bar soap directly over the Internet?

I don't believe that Unilever had any special insight when it announced its advertising plan. Instead, I think that the company acted from a general sense of urgency—a gut-level drive to do something rather than nothing at all. That something turned out to be a public commitment to spend $50 million.

Unilever is not alone in feeling pressed to take action—any action—on the Internet. Pillsbury, for example, created a Web advertising campaign featuring a click-on Pillsbury Doughboy, and Procter & Gamble has assembled an industry consortium to make the Internet a better medium for brand advertising. All of these moves succeeded in creating media attention from publications like *Advertising Age* and *The Wall Street Journal.*

Yet the leaders of these consumer companies know, and Technographics data clearly shows, that most of the people who bake muffins, wash clothes, and buy diapers aren't on the Internet. It is hard to make the case that these traditional companies have advanced their brands with consumers at all through their Internet activities. But with the investment community so focused on the Internet, it would be tough to take the position that your company has considered the situation and decided to do nothing.

Unfortunately, no matter how good a company's Web site is, it will not reach many Sidelined Citizens. Laggard consumers cannot afford technology. With a median income of less than $20,000, these consumers would have to spend 5 percent of their gross income in order to buy a PC. And unlike low-income optimists, the pessimists rarely have access to the Internet through a workplace computer (Figure 2).

Many work in blue- and pink-collar jobs. They are gas station attendants, teacher's aides, nurses, store clerks, receptionists, and road repair workers. Almost a third are retired.

But marketers face a bigger problem than Sidelined Citizens' level of income. These consumers are pessimistic about technology. Even if they could afford a home PC, most probably wouldn't buy one. And if they had a PC, it is unlikely that these consumers would use it for on-line shopping (see Figure 3).

After all, fewer than 50 percent of Sidelined Citizens use the automated teller machines at their bank for making deposits and withdrawals. That technology is free, and it has been around for more than twenty years.

The question, then, is, how can companies whose consumer Technographics put them at risk of falling into the Laggard Trap avoid it? The answer: They must match their Internet strategies to the Technographic segmentation of their *mainstream* consumers, then pull along the laggards as best they can. Companies that serve a large group of low-income pessimists can choose one of two paths for centering their Internet strategy:

1. Move up the income scale, to *high-income pessimists*; or
2. Focus across the attitude scale, toward *low-income optimists*.

Let's look at how such a strategy works in action. Take the case of Fingerhut Corporation. This $1.6 billion company sells housewares and clothing to mainly moderate-income consumers through

	Low-Income Pessimists	Overall Population
Demographics		
Male	**37%**	49%
Under 30	**11%**	14%
30 to 44	**27%**	35%
45 and over	**62%**	51%
Median age	**53**	45
At least some college	**21%**	47%
Married	**44%**	54%
Median income	**$17,000**	$36,000
Children under 18	**28%**	34%
Technology Habits		
Have additional phone line	**13%**	25%
Have fax machine	**9%**	21%
Have pager	**19%**	29%
Have a cellular phone	**25%**	46%
Have a palm computer	**4%**	6%
Own a PC	**22%**	48%
Use a computer at work	**18%**	47%
On-line Activities		
Go on-line regularly	**10%**	33%
Purchase on-line	**2%**	9%
Do financial transactions on-line	**0%**	2%

Source: Forrester Research, Inc.

Figure 2 A Technographics Profile of Low-Income Pessimists

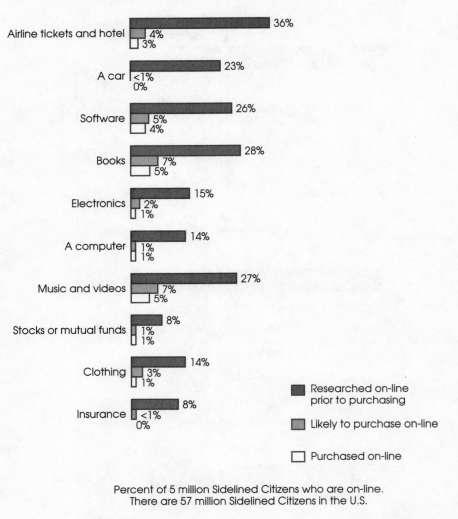

Airline tickets and hotel — 36%, 4%, 3%

A car — 23%, <1%, 0%

Software — 26%, 5%, 4%

Books — 28%, 7%, 5%

Electronics — 15%, 2%, 1%

A computer — 14%, 1%, 1%

Music and videos — 27%, 7%, 5%

Stocks or mutual funds — 8%, 1%, 1%

Clothing — 14%, 3%, 1%

Insurance — 8%, <1%, 0%

■ Researched on-line prior to purchasing

■ Likely to purchase on-line

□ Purchased on-line

Percent of 5 million Sidelined Citizens who are on-line.
There are 57 million Sidelined Citizens in the U.S.

Source: Forrester Research, Inc.

Figure 3 Products Sidelined Citizens Research and Purchase On-line

twenty-five different mail-order catalogs. Fingerhut's Technographic profile reveals a classic Laggard Trap distribution: A quarter of the company's consumers are Sidelined Citizens, but only 8 percent are Fast Forwards (see Figure 4). Fingerhut might easily have concluded that it should wait two or three years before investing in electronic commerce.

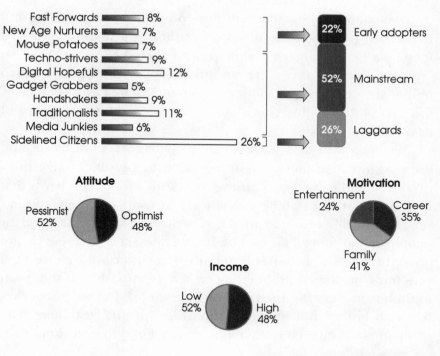

Source: 1998 Fall Mediamark Research, Inc.

Figure 4 Technographics of Fingerhut Consumers

Instead, Fingerhut has avoided the Laggard Trap by focusing on the part of its consumer base most likely to be on-line now—low-income optimists. Gadget Grabbers, Digital Hopefuls, and Techno-strivers make up 26 percent of Fingerhut's consumer base.[1] Rather than try to move all its traditional catalog consumers to the Internet at once, Fingerhut has opted to make a series of investments in new Internet companies that serve the interests of upwardly mobile young consumers.

The first of these affiliates, The Zone Network, publishes Mountain Zone. This site targets skiers, rock climbers, and outdoor photographers—a notably well-educated, young group of consumers. A second Fingerhut affiliate, FreeShop, lists free offers and trial incentives over the Internet—a direct answer to low-income optimists' search for value and entertainment on-line. A third,

71

Andysauction.com, liquidates distressed inventory for clothing and household-goods sellers—offering consumers a deal on branded merchandise. Finally, Fingerhut created thehut.com, which offers "cool stuff at low prices." These Internet sites let Fingerhut reach millions more young consumers each month than it ever could have if it had pinned its Internet strategy purely on Internet versions of its traditional catalogs.

Yet Fingerhut also plans to fully engage its mainstream and even laggard consumers on-line as soon as possible. Fingerhut's president and CEO, Will Lansing, puts it this way: "My view is that in the end, it's not going to matter that some consumers aren't very technically oriented to begin with. The barriers caused by people not owning PCs or not having the skills to use PCs are going to fall. The Internet is about the relationship that we have with our consumers and building on that relationship. If they want to do business on the Internet, we'll be there." Indeed, Fingerhut has built lasting and strong relationships with its customers. The company's average consumer has been a Fingerhut customer for seven years.

What about the possibility that many Sidelined Citizens will never go on-line? Lansing doesn't let this slow him—or Fingerhut—down. He explains, "In mail order, the market topped out at about 60 percent of consumers. Maybe the Internet will top out somewhere around 60 percent, too. I don't know. But I do know that we've already reached a point where it makes sense to go after our consumers on the Internet. Right now, 35 percent of our buyers have PCs, but 65 percent can get on the Internet either from work or at the library, if they can't go on from home. If there's been any delay in marketing to our traditional customers to shop on-line with us, it's because we don't feel we're ready rather than a concern that they won't be ready."

Fingerhut is actually a key player in helping to get mainstream consumers and laggards on-line. The company's handtech.com site is already among the top one hundred retailers of PCs. Handtech.com sells computers for $1,000 or less. Just as important, Fingerhut's credit arm often finances the computer purchase. "We're really good at understanding the credit-constrained consumer," says Lansing. "The fact that we can lend money in the sub-prime market fuels the move of moderate-income consumers to the Internet."

As it turns out, during our research, Forrester collected information from thousands of Fingerhut consumers directly. An interview with one of them, named Kay, offers a good insight into what the Internet looks like from the laggards' point of view—and how a company like Fingerhut can help these consumers overcome the obstacles that are preventing them from shopping on-line.

Kay lives with her divorced daughter and three grandchildren in South Carolina. Although she worked years ago inputting data into a mainframe computer, Kay, now in her late fifties, stays home to help out her daughter, who works as a nurse. Kay's early workplace experiences with computers were not unpleasant. In fact, she says it was sort of interesting to learn about them. But since she stopped working more than a decade ago, Kay hasn't touched a computer. Recent news reports about computer viruses and hackers have made Kay suspicious of technology. "I have heard that if you have a computer, someone could tap in," she tells us.

Despite these privacy concerns, and even though they can barely afford one, Kay thinks her family still *might* end up getting a PC for the children, who are ten, eight, and seven years old. Though neither Kay nor her daughter is attracted to technology, they care deeply about the children and recognize that without a computer their kids are at a disadvantage in school. This sentiment is not at all unusual among low-income pessimists—the majority of these consumers are females, and 28 percent are currently raising children.

We asked Kay if she would ever shop on-line. "No, probably not," she answers. Kay says she likes shopping in person because it gets her out of the house. "What about at Fingerhut?" we ask. This gets a different response from Kay. "If Fingerhut went on the Internet, then I would, too. I buy a lot from them, and it would be very convenient to go and put my order in myself." Kay evidently does not know that Fingerhut is already on-line. We ask her about her privacy concerns—isn't she worried that someone might tap in? Kay replies, "I would still go to Fingerhut. I like them, and I don't mind anyone knowing that I shop from them."

Kay's personal responses reflect the results of the broader Technographics study. While Sidelined Citizens face significant obstacles to going on-line, they should not be written off as a lost cause. Companies serving these consumers should instead focus on helping them get on-line. After all, Kay is more likely to respond to an invitation from Fingerhut to shop on-line than she is to answer the call of any Internet service provider.

What do consumers like Kay need to go on-line? Above all, they need an inexpensive, maybe even free, personal computer. Recently, companies such as eMachines have begun offering PCs for as little as $600. This company has already made an impact, and not just among high-income consumers, who often buy a cheap second PC for their children, but also among low-income consumers. In the first six months of operations, eMachines sold more than five hundred thousand PCs—about half of them to households that had never before owned a PC.

In addition, a number of start-up companies, including FreePC, Empire.net, NetZero, and DirectWeb, are experimenting with offering Internet services on the cable television model—the price of the hardware is included in the monthly access fee, and/or advertising funds a significant part of the cost. Companies like Fingerhut and Unilever do better by supporting this kind of effort to get people with moderate incomes on-line than by buying Web banner ads that reach fewer of their target consumers.

Consumers like Kay need also need a motive to go on-line. You might expect the fact that Internet stores often undercut the prices of retailers would be reason enough. Having limited resources, Sidelined Citizens ought to be more likely than others to clip coupons and switch brands for a discount. However, our Technographics research indicates that these consumers are actually not much more likely than anyone else is to spend their money carefully. Internet companies would have better results with a different approach, a family-oriented one. Sixty-three percent of Sidelined Citizens are women, who can be motivated around family needs, particularly the education of children and grandchildren.

BEING REALISTIC ABOUT THE LAGGARDS

While it would be a mistake to ignore the needs of laggard consumers, companies must also accept the fact that many of them probably will never go on-line. Only 10 percent connected to the Internet in 1999, and Forrester's rosiest outlook suggests that no more than 30 percent will do so. Even if they were all connected, Sidelined Citizens account for less than one-twelfth of personal disposable income, so they'll never spend as much as other Technographic groups.

Large consumer companies must be careful not to let the presence of laggards in their existing consumer base prevent them from seizing Internet opportunities aimed purely at other Technographics groups. Far better to accept the facts that high-income consumers are going to do business differently than low-income consumers do and that optimists will be different from pessimists, then build an Internet strategy that addresses the Technographics segmentation among consumers. Large traditional companies should take three steps to avoid the Laggard Trap:

- **Segment for individual brands and products**. Rather than try to construct a single Internet strategy, corporations should consider each brand separately. The Technographics of Pillsbury's entire product line, for example, would mask the important differences between consumers of Green Giant frozen vegetables, a mainstream product, and Häagen-Dazs, the company's premium ice cream. For automobile makers, the Technographic differences between brands like Ford and General Motors are less significant than the distinctions among different vehicle types. Recreational vehicles and trucks exhibit a

Laggard Trap pattern, whereas sport utility vehicles appeal to higher-income consumers, and motorcycles appeal mainly to technology optimists.[2]

- **Pursue a multichannel Internet strategy.** Just as they must for mainstream consumers, companies must allow laggards to buy wherever they're most comfortable. Consider the situation of Maybelline cosmetics. Maybelline's Technographics lean toward high-income pessimists but also include a large group of Sidelined Citizens (see Figure 5).

This is the pattern you might expect of a company that sells a medium-priced product mostly to women. Maybelline's optimistic consumers, 46 percent of the total, require sales and service on the Web from Internet drugstores as well as from

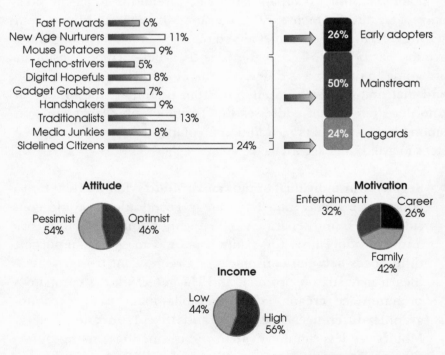

Source: 1998 Fall Mediamark Research, Inc.

Figure 5 Technographics of Maybelline Consumers

Maybelline. But the pessimists will probably be buying at the corner drugstore for a long time to come.

- **Help along slower mainstream consumers and laggards.** While they may move more slowly to the Internet than other consumers, low-income pessimists can be brought to the Internet by companies they know and trust—especially if those companies are willing, as Fingerhut is, to invest in moving the relationship on-line.

CONCLUSIONS

This chapter completes Part One of *Now or Never*—Understanding Internet Consumers. In the battle of the Internet, even though start-ups have seized the lead with early adopters, it is not too late for traditional companies to compete successfully. Early adopters have only just begun to shop on-line, and mainstream consumers have yet to purchase en masse.

As the body of Internet consumers shifts from being almost exclusively early adopters to include mainstream and even laggard consumers, traditional companies are likely to gain the upper hand. This is because mainstream consumers naturally gravitate toward companies they know and brands they like. To cope with this new consumer dynamic, start-up companies must become easier for consumers to find in the physical world. In most cases, this will require promoting their new brands through traditional media.

For traditional companies that serve a large number of consumers, winning the battle for Internet consumers will require separating optimists from pessimists. Traditional companies that treat consumers as one homogeneous group will find it difficult to generate much business from their Internet activities. Instead, companies should consider the Technographics of each product line and brand within their portfolio to determine their approach to the Internet and their investment priorities. Pessimists require encouragement to go on-line, while optimists already expect full service via the Internet.

But having ready consumers is only the first skirmish. To win the Internet battle, start-up companies must not only sell—they must sell profitably. Traditional companies must find a way to compete on the Internet without wrecking their existing business. In Part Two we'll look at how the Internet has changed the competitive environment and what that means for both types of companies.

PART 2

Exploiting Internet Business Models

CHAPTER 6

The Internet's Impact on Competition

As more and more consumers—particularly mainstream consumers—go on-line in the next few years, the competition between traditional companies and dotcoms is going to change considerably. As we saw in Part One, wider consumer adoption will raise the importance of known brands and will require companies to sell and service consumers consistently across on-line and off-line venues. Consumer Technographics shows that early adopters have different attitudes toward technology, resources, and motivations to go on-line than do consumers in the mainstream and laggard groups. To do business on-line, later consumers require a level of familiarity and affordability that early adopters do not.

In Part Two, we look at the battle for Internet consumers through a different camera angle. Having examined the beliefs and motives that underlie consumer activity, we will focus now on the business models that drive the competition between traditional companies and dotcoms. The question becomes, How can companies exploit the new business models made possible by the Internet? Part Two explores what is in store for consumer companies once the Internet becomes as widely popular as the automobile.

To say that the Internet has made consumer businesses more competitive is an understatement. The Internet has stripped away many of the barriers to competition that businesses used to take for granted—barriers such as geographic separation, lack of information, and poor communication. While the idea that the Internet intensifies competition is no surprise, it is worth taking a moment to examine how—and to consider what will happen as Internet commerce reaches critical mass. At $10 billion, the Internet is a sideshow in the consumer economy. At $100 billion, the Internet will significantly alter traditional consumer industries.

At Forrester, we call the post-Internet competitive environment *Dynamic Trade*. As the Internet matures, consumer markets will become far more fluid and responsive to changes in supply and demand than they have been in the past—in other words, more dynamic. Because the Internet tears down the barriers that have limited competition, companies will perceive a marked increase in rivalry and, in most cases, lower prices. In Dynamic Trade:

> *The Internet makes actual supply and demand more apparent, so prices naturally fall to their lowest competitive point and vary more as demand shifts.*

The scope of change that Dynamic Trade will cause in consumer industries is not easy to grasp. But companies that fail to understand and adjust to Dynamic Trade will lose control of their prices, revenue streams, and profits as more consumers shop on-line.

THE INTERNET INCREASES APPARENT SUPPLY

Consider how the Internet affects supply from the point of view of the consumer. When a buyer seeks a product, whether it is information such as news or hard goods like groceries, they go to the market. But the market is only as large as the one that a consumer can reasonably address. To an isolated villager, the "market" is limited to what is piled up in the stalls of local merchants. Similarly, when a woman drives in her sedan to the mall, she chooses a blouse from among the stores in the mall. If she wants to, she can drive another forty-five minutes to a discount store like TJ Maxx or Frugal Fannies, where it is possible (though she can't be sure beforehand) that she'll find the exact same blouse at 50 percent off. But most women won't take the time to go find out.

In the cases of both the villager and the mall shopper, the actual supply of whatever they were seeking is many times larger than the supply around which they must make their purchase decisions. However, it simply isn't practical for consumers to locate and include all of the actual supply when making their decisions. Instead, consumers make their purchases from the supply they can easily find—the *apparent supply* (see Figure 1).

While there is no evidence that the Internet increases the actual supply of goods in any consumer market, it clearly increases the apparent supply. Going on-line requires a considerable effort from consumers. And as we saw in Part One, not all consumers greet this challenge with enthusiasm. Once on-line, however, consumers can visit both upscale shops and discounters without moving an inch. In

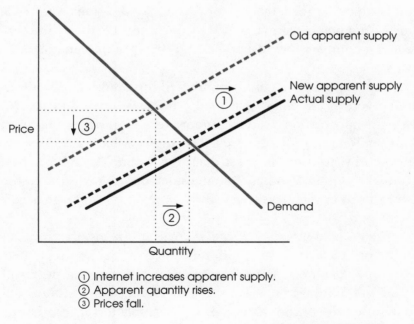

① Internet increases apparent supply.
② Apparent quantity rises.
③ Prices fall.

Source: Forrester Research, Inc.

Figure 1 The Internet Increases Apparent Supply

addition, new price-comparison engines sift through hundreds of Web sites, searching for the best price on a given item. As a result, the Internet is driving up the quantity of goods that consumers can see and driving down prices.

To illustrate this, Forrester went shopping with mySimon, DealTime, and Bottomdollar.com, just three of the many price-comparison robots now available to consumers on the Internet. We found a 37 percent price difference in the cost of one music CD and large gaps in consumer electronics and kitchen equipment as well. Not only that, but the Internet sites as a group undercut the retail stores by an average of more than 15 percent (see Figure 2).

The increase in apparent supply is most pronounced when consumers cross national borders in their on-line shopping expeditions. They discover, for example, that a PC from a U.S. site is priced 30 to 40 percent less than a nearly identical model offered in Germany. Often in cases like this, the higher price actually reflects a tariff levied on imports. However, it also could reflect a less competitive local market for certain goods—a market that supports a higher retail mark-up. On the Internet, these differences become completely transparent, and usually unacceptable, to the consumer.

The increase in apparent supply and the resulting price declines have been most remarkable in the information industries. Many types of information used to support very high prices because the information was difficult to get. The Internet has made it easy and inexpensive to transmit most data. For example, in 1994, people paid $300 a month to get real-time stock quotes delivered to them. Now this information is free with most on-line brokerage accounts (see Figure 3).

High apparent supply causes real problems for companies whose products are sold at different prices in markets separated by geography or information. This is not to say that real price differences will not exist between, say, a high-end model of a car and a low-end model of the same make. It is simply to suggest that price differences based on poor information or geographic distance won't stand up very well in the Internet economy.

ON-LINE PRICE COMPARISON RESULTS

Product	Company	Price	Price quoted in retail stores
Compact disc	TotalE	$13.58	
Dave Matthews:	CD Connection	$13.30	Tower Records
Before These	Pentagon	$11.99	$13.99
Crowded Streets	Buy.com	$9.94	
Blender	HelpFindit	$64.46	
Cuisinart Cordless	Cooking.com	$59.99	Macy's
Rechargeable	The Internet Kitchen	$55.00	$69.99
Hand Blender	Brandsmall	$54.90	
Personal digital	Mobile Planet	$449.95	
assistant	CompUSA	$429.95	CompUSA
3Com PalmPilot V	PCMall.com	$399.99	$449.99
Connected Organizer	Egghead.com	$362.79	
	eCost.com	$348.94	

On-line price comparison results from
mySimon, DealTime, and
Bottomdollar.com, June 24, 1999.

Source: Forrester Research, Inc.

Figure 2 Price Comparison on the Internet

PRICES RESPOND TO CURRENT DEMAND

In addition to reducing prices to their lowest point, the Internet is tying prices more closely to actual demand. Before the Internet, companies had no way of aggregating information about consumer demand. In fact, the only markets where demand was really visible were exchanges such as the Chicago Board of Trade, for commodities, or the New York Stock Exchange. The participants in these markets were mostly corporations, not individuals.

Computer networks have made it possible for a company to see how much consumer demand exists for a given product at any time. Measuring consumer demand is really no different from gathering

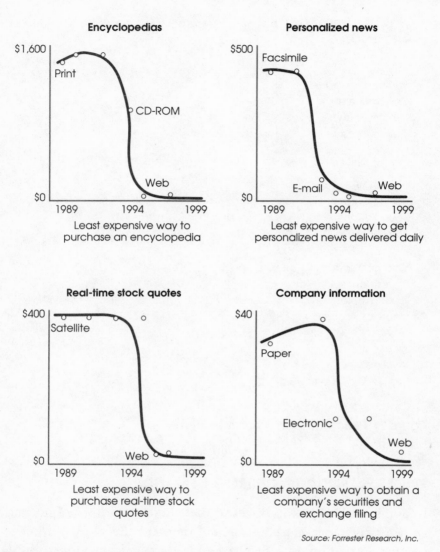

Source: Forrester Research, Inc.

Figure 3 Prices Fall on the Internet

point-of-sale data, as grocery stores and other retailers do now. However, most traditional point-of-sale retail data is delivered in printed reports a month or more after sales are made. On the Internet, companies can collect, and act on, live point-of-sale data. This kind of information has been rare in the past, found only in a few selling venues such as live auctions and television home shopping. While most on-line retailers do not yet gather live sales data, Web sites are capable of offering retailers a minute-by-minute view of what is selling and for how much.

I understood for the first time the power of this kind of information when I went on a tour of the Home Shopping Network's operations facility in Florida. My host took me first to the television studios, which were broadcasting live. There sat the models you see on TV selling dolls and jewelry. But these are no ordinary models—they are saleswomen, paid on commission. To help them sell, an information screen is located directly below the studio's TV cameras. This screen shows exactly how many consumers are currently buying the item for sale at the price they're offering. The saleswoman has the authority to change the price or to move on to another item based on her judgment of this live sales data. Her goal is to maximize the profits of her two-hour television slot.

The way the sales information system works is truly amazing. We left the TV studio and walked down the hall into a warehouse that must have covered an acre of ground. In it sat hundreds of telephone representatives taking orders and inputting them into Home Shopping's computer systems. The computers aggregated this information—in real time—and sent it to the screen in the studio so the saleswoman could see immediately if her pitch was working or not.

I believe that the studios at Home Shopping Network offer an idea of what selling on-line will be like when the Internet reaches critical mass. While the legions of telephone representatives and the woman on television probably won't be a part of it, the aggregation of live sales data and the benefit of responding immediately with pricing and merchandise adjustments will. Rather than try to guess in advance what mix of products and prices will sell, suppliers will *feel* their way by measuring the *current demand* in the marketplace.

The Internet will go much further in finding consumer demand than television home shopping ever could. Amazon.com began two years ago to generate and measure demand *in advance of sales* by taking prepublication orders for upcoming books and music CDs. Advance selling is not new, but in the past, only large buyers such as distributors ordered enough to make it worth doing. The Internet has made it possible to aggregate all the advance orders of millions of consumers in one place.

The Internet also makes it possible for consumers to express demand and let companies respond to them. In traditional businesses, this kind of "request for proposal" exists almost exclusively in the business-to-business environment, where the number of buyers and sellers in any market is smaller. Computer networks, though, allow this same process to occur in consumer markets. At Priceline, for example, consumers can name a price at which they would like to travel between two destinations on a certain date. Airlines bid to fill the consumer's order. The same type of transaction takes place in the on-line auto market. Consumers describe in detail the car they seek and ask dealers to quote.

As the Internet reaches critical mass, information systems will actually change the way companies measure demand and set prices. In the past, suppliers set the market agenda, determining which products to sell and at what price. The successful companies were those that did a good job of estimating future demand. Of course, no company ever estimated demand exactly right, so gaps existed. Sometimes, companies missed the opportunity to sell, when demand ran higher than available supply. Other times, they made more than the market wanted and had to write off inventory. Using primitive tools like monthly retail reports, companies tried to adjust to demand, but their ability to react was limited (see Figure 4).

On the Internet, companies will measure and respond to *current demand:* what consumers want now. As they do, they will change the dynamics of competition. When consumers set the agenda, it is more important for companies to be able to *respond quickly* than it is for them to *predict well.* In Dynamic Trade, companies that can adjust the prices and quantities of goods—their supply—more closely to consumers' current demand will succeed. This eliminates the gaps between what consumers want and what companies can offer them.

Take, for example, how the Internet is changing the way that the toy industry manages peak demand during the holiday season. No one knows for sure in advance which toy will turn out to be the

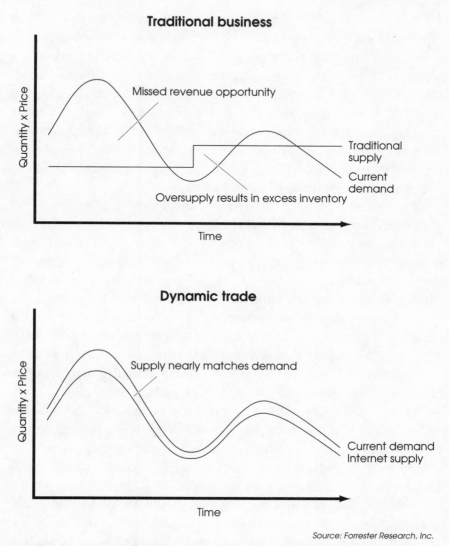

Figure 4 Dynamic Trade Matches Supply with Demand

hot buy of the holidays, so it is tough to plan toy production. Toy companies must make enough so that many people can buy a toy if it does become popular, but not so many that the market becomes flooded and consumers lose interest. Every year, there is a gap between the supply of the hot toy and its demand.

When Tickle Me Elmo was the rage in 1996, newspapers reported stories about parents waiting hours in line or shoving each other aside in the stores to get hold of the toy. Shopkeepers rationed Elmos—"one per customer, please," read the hastily taped-up signs. But Elmo's price at retail never changed, and the supplier never made enough Elmos to satisfy consumer demand. If a black market did develop, it was hard to locate. In 1998, when Furby was the hot toy, early-adopter consumers avoided the crush in stores by turning to Internet auctions, where Furby's price, normally $30 to $40 at retail, raced up to more than $300.

The Furby experience offers just a small taste of what lies ahead as competitive consumer markets move on-line. The seasonal run-up in the price of Furby occurred at a time when fewer than 10 percent of all consumers were on-line buyers and less than 1 percent of toys were sold electronically. Imagine what will happen in 2010, when on-line buying accounts for a quarter of the toy market.

In purely competitive markets, price is the main mechanism for bringing supply in line with demand—and so it is on the Internet. Therefore, consumer companies must learn to use pricing as a live market mechanism. When current demand is high, Furby's maker, Hasbro, might decide to raise prices rather than make more. Alternately, the expression of significant demand at $300 for Furby in November could induce the company to produce more in order to manage the "hot toy" premium downward. In either case, the sudden visibility of a market-determined price for Furby gives Hasbro more ways to maximize its profits.

The toy industry is not the only one to be affected by changes in current demand. In fact, any consumer industry that operates on a seasonal pattern—like fashion—or that is characterized by temporary "hits"—such as movies and music—or that focuses on events—like sports and entertainment—will experience similar dynamics on the Internet.

Retailers that have managed gaps between supply and demand using blunt tools such as end-of-season sales and layaway plans will adjust their prices far more often in response to Internet competition. Event promoters that have sold tickets through the orderly, if expensive, system of box office sales plus Ticketmaster will require new distribution systems that let consumers bid up the price of popular event seats and pay less for unpopular ones. Ditto for recorded music, software, and movies: If electronic distribution is cheap, perhaps the official price should fall, allowing unit sales to expand. The existence of illegal markets for these goods in part reflects the fact that companies have not served the demand that exists at lower prices.

Companies that fail to manage current demand in the Dynamic Trade environment will find their products trading over the Internet at prices they never intended—free in some cases, six or eight times the list price in others. But even companies whose products do not experience such wild swings can use current demand to improve margins. In retailing, where profits traditionally are very low, current demand measurement offers a way to offset the pricing effects of higher apparent supply (see Figure 5).

DYNAMIC TRADE REQUIRES INTERNET BUSINESSES TO SCALE FAST

In a world of expanding apparent supply, consumers are attracted to Web sites that offer a complete range of products. At the same time, companies that wish to track current demand must have sufficient volume to generate a composite view of the market for the goods they sell. Both factors indicate that Internet businesses must achieve a certain scale in order to be competitive.

But beyond those strategic indications, the cost structure of Internet businesses also makes the case for the emergence of a few, very large companies. In order to compete, Internet companies must scale up fast in terms of the number of products they sell and the number of consumers they serve. This requires Internet businesses to build a consumer base fast and to invest in technology that enables them to measure and respond to consumer activities. In Dynamic Trade, the customer base and the technology infrastructure become the key assets of a consumer business.

Unfortunately, neither of these key assets is tangible. Consumers come and go from site to site—no one "owns" an Internet consumer.

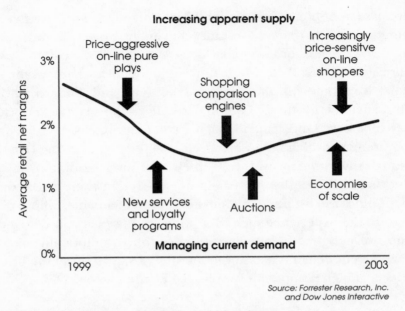

Figure 5 Price Pressure Shrinks Retail Margins

And while technology investment results in some tangibles, such as computers and prepaid network connections, the bulk of the value lies in intangible technology know-how. Companies that know how to measure demand, react to consumer requests, and deliver effective service to customers will win on the Internet. As a rule:

> *Dynamic Trade favors companies that build economies of scale around intangible assets.*

Let's look at how Internet companies build the key assets of Dynamic Trade: customer base and technology infrastructure.

Traditional companies built their consumer bases largely through television advertising. Sales by companies that established a trusted brand far surpassed those of competitors that did not brand. Once built, the customer base had to be maintained through ongoing communication. But that marketing expense was fairly discretionary. When the chips were down, companies could always cut back on advertising for a while—and they did. The advertising business shows this truth most plainly, booming in good times and contracting whenever the economy slows.

For Internet businesses, marketing behaves as a fixed cost—a cost that companies cannot decide to trim, especially during the early days. Moreover, this cost expands as a step function rather than smoothly in line with sales.

What is the marketing cost for Internet companies? Some advertise on television, it's true, but most do not. Instead, they pay to place their company's name and a link back to their site on the most popular Internet directories, or "portal" sites. And unlike TV advertising deals, the portal placements, as they are called in the industry, usually cover two to five years at a time. These deals cost the buyer anywhere from $5 million to $500 million dollars. Over the last three years, the number and cost of these deals has been increasing (see Figure 6).

I had dinner with a client who had just signed a portal deal, and I asked him what he thought about it. "We were lucky to get the deal," he told me, "because [our competitor] was also in there bidding. It would have killed us if they had won. It means we're going to be losing money for the next two years, but I think it will keep us in the running on customer acquisition." His comment illustrates the difference between Internet companies' view of the marketing budget and traditional companies' view of it. To the Internet manager, portal deals are not so much about building a brand as they are about building a *sales distribution channel*.

It is only natural to look at the Internet and conclude that since everyone is connected, your customers can get to you. A more useful view, however, is that the network allows *you* to connect to *them*—wherever they are. Rather than seeing your Web site as a single, huge point of sale, imagine for a moment that it is merely the back office of the Internet business. The points of sale number in the thousands, or even millions, as you distribute your name and sales links to other Internet sites and eventually onto consumers' desktops, palm computers, and telephones.

To acquire a consumer base, Internet companies expand their points of sale as quickly as possible. That is why they pay so much for

Annual total value of announced portal deals

1997	1998	1999
$244	$719	$856 (first 6 mos.)

On-line retailer	Internet portal	Total contract value (millions)	Term of contract (years)	Annual value (millions)
1999 (first six months)				
FirstUSA	AOL	$500	5	$100
MBNA	Go	$100	3	$33
eBay	AOL	$75	4	$19
DrKoop.com	Go	$57	3	$19
WebMD	Lycos	$53	3	$18
AutoConnect	AOL	$17	2.2	$8
PlanetRx	AOL	$15	3	$5
CNET	AOL	$15	2.5	$6
HealthQuick.com	AOL	$10	2	$5
iTurf	AOL	$8	2	$4
Averages		**$85**	**3.0**	**$29**
1998				
Bank One	Excite	$125	4	$31
FirstUSA	MSN	$90	5	$18
Intuit	AOL	$30	3	$10
DLJDirect	AOL	$25	2	$13
E*TRADE	AOL	$25	2	$13
Waterhouse	AOL	$25	2	$13
Ameritrade	AOL	$25	2	$13
CBS Sportsline	AOL	$23	3	$8
Fleet	Lycos	$23	3	$8
CD Now	Lycos	$19	3	$6
Averages		**$41**	**2.9**	**$14**
1997				
CUC Int'l	AOL	$50	3	$17
Barnesandnoble.com	AOL	$40	4	$10
Preview Travel	AOL	$32	5	$6
cybermeals	AOL	$30	4	$8
1-800 Flowers	AOL	$25	4	$6
Amazon.com	AOL	19	3	$6
N2K	AOL	$18	3	$6
Preview Travel	Excite	$15	5	$3
Internet Liquidators	AOL	$10	2	$5
(16 companies)	Excite	$5	2.5	$2
Averages		**$24**	**3.6**	**$7**

NOTE: Yahoo! does not release details of its marketing deals.

Source: Forrester Research, Inc.

Figure 6 Top Internet Marketing Deals

portal deals. It also explains their investments in affiliate marketing. CDNow and Amazon pioneered affiliate marketing, which means that anyone with a Web site can sign up as a sales affiliate and get between 5 percent and 15 percent of the price of books and CDs sold through their site. Becoming an affiliate is ideal for small businesspeople who want to earn some money on the side—and it also adds customers and revenues to Amazon and CDNow.

Building a customer base large enough to compete in Dynamic Trade means investing to build an Internet sales distribution channel. But once this sales distribution channel is in place, marketing begins to decline as a percent of sales in most Internet businesses. In other words, companies experience economies of scale around the distribution channel. A look at Amazon's marketing expenses illustrates this pattern (see Figure 7).

Back in 1996, marketing accounted for 39 percent of net sales. By 1998, it had fallen to 22 percent. This is not to suggest that Amazon spent less on marketing—in fact, the company spent more in each successive quarter. However, as the Internet sales distribution channel grew, it generated sales growth that more than covered the increases in marketing.

Technology investments also represent a large fixed cost that

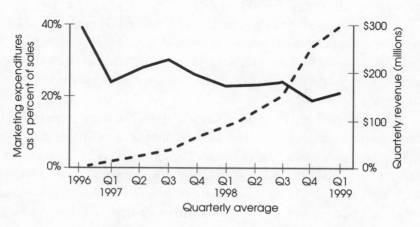

Source: Forrester Research, Inc. and EDGAR Online, Inc.

Figure 7 Quarterly Marketing Expenditures at Amazon

Internet companies must bear in order to play in the market. Sometimes, the importance of adequate investment in technology is difficult for managers of traditional companies to accept. After all, large companies are used to smooth and predictable information technology expenses. It is not atypical to see technology expenditure at just 2 or 3 percent of sales for year after year in major corporations.

However, for Internet businesses, the technology is the business. Without its Web site, a company like eBay doesn't exist! The performance of the servers, the layout of the Web site, the design of the pages, how the e-mail system responds, and other features of the software system all define what the Internet company is in the eyes of consumers and how well it can serve them. Not least, companies must be able to monitor their own Web sites as the Internet reaches critical mass and as companies begin to measure and act on current demand.

Thus, we don't see technology expenses at 3 percent of sales in Internet companies; we see investments four or five times that large. In addition, Web site technology expenditures do not remain stable as a percent of sales; they vary tremendously. For Internet companies, servers, software licenses, and the staff that mans the machines must periodically be upgraded to the next level of capacity. This creates a step function in technology investment and makes technology a highly variable part of the income statement. eBay's financials show this pattern well (see Figure 8).

Technology varied between 15 percent and 35 percent of sales over eight successive quarters. Each time the company upgraded its Web site, added more technical people, or acquired technology through acquisition, its cost of sales and technology development jumped.

Taken together, the marketing and technology expenditures that characterize Internet businesses yield a very interesting pattern. Building a sales distribution channel attracts consumers who flood the Web site. So the technology infrastructure must be upgraded to deal with the new demands upon it. Because it makes sense to upgrade beyond the current load, the upgrade creates a temporary excess capacity. Therefore, the company must acquire even more consumers. And so these two fixed costs spiral upward

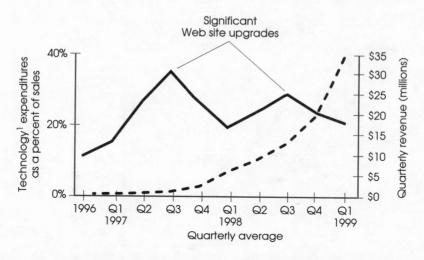

1. Technology includes cost of sales, which consists of eBay's Web site and its ongoing support, as well as R&D, which consists of site development.

Source: Forrester Research. Inc. and EDGAR Online, Inc.

Figure 8   Quarterly Technology Expenditures at eBay

together in a double helix that represents a significant fixed investment in intangibles (see Figure 9).

The goods news about this upward cost spiral is that it generates an important momentum in revenue growth. As more consumers visit a site and buy there, a company gets better at measuring and delivering what consumers want. The bad news is that the double helix almost invariably generates losses in the short run. Companies might be able to cover just the technology, or just the marketing, but rarely both at first. An Internet company must grow to achieve a scale that will leverage its fixed investments in intangibles.

Unfortunately, companies that fail to invest adequately in either sales distribution or technology lose momentum in customer acquisition. Some companies put all their effort into technology. However, without a sales distribution channel, the site ends up as a "best-kept secret" that never generates enough revenues to cover its costs. Companies that spend all their energies on marketing but neglect technology attract a large number of consumers to a site that is slow

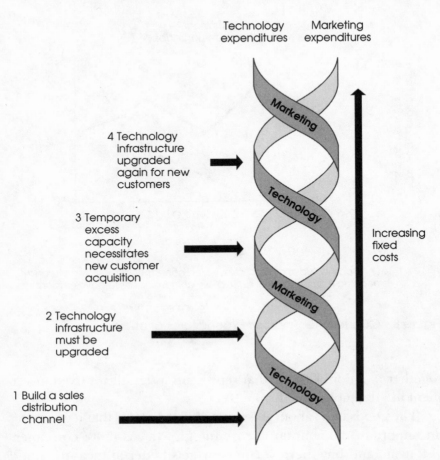

Technology
expenditures

Marketing
expenditures

Marketing

Technology

Marketing

Technology

4 Technology
infrastructure
upgraded
again for new
customers

3 Temporary
excess
capacity
necessitates
new customer
acquisition

2 Technology
infrastructure
must be
upgraded

1 Build a sales
distribution
channel

Increasing
fixed
costs

Source: Forrester Research, Inc.

Figure 9 Marketing and Technology Expenditures
Build on Each Other

and doesn't work very well. In both cases, the result is that early revenue growth tapers off and can be hard to jump-start again (see Figure 10).

ZEROING OUT MARGINAL COST

For companies that do invest adequately in their Web site, the effects on marginal costs can be nothing short of astonishing. Once

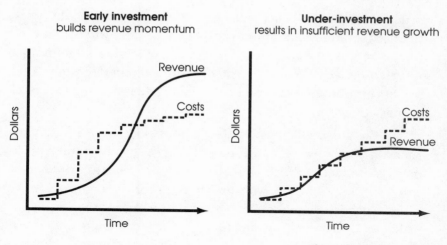

Figure 10 The Impact of Investment Choices in Technology and Distribution

an Internet business achieves a large enough scale, marginal costs fall by an order of magnitude. In other words, we're not talking about a 25 percent decline in marginal costs; we're talking about marginal costs that are *one-tenth* as large as they were before the Internet. Once the technology infrastructure is built, the cost of adding another customer account or offering a new product in an on-line store is very, very low. Forrester's research indicates that marginal costs fall most dramatically in four areas:

1: **Cost of promotion**. Once an Internet company acquires a customer, the cost of offering that customer a special product or deal falls dramatically. Take, for example, the cost that a company like L.L. Bean or Williams Sonoma incurs when it sends its catalog to customers each quarter. A typical catalog run, say twelve million households, costs 70 cents a catalog.[1] On-line, the same merchant can e-mail the same twelve million people with a link back to a Web site where they can actually buy the products for 10 cents a household—one-seventh of the cost of the direct-mail promotion.

2: **Cost of taking orders**. For companies that take their orders by telephone, as most catalog merchants do, the typical order costs $3.90,[2] which reflects mainly the time of the telephone operator. The same order taken on-line, where the customer inputs the order information, billing, and shipping instructions, costs an average of 20 cents. Even better, when consumers input their own orders, the error rate is half as only large as that of telephone operators.[3]

3: **Cost of market reach**. Retail stores like Toys "R" Us and Kmart typically serve consumers in a twenty-mile radius, and many stores serve much smaller areas. Retail stores are expensive to set up and stock with products. Once the company saturates a particular geography, it must set up another store in order to serve new consumers. The Internet breaks this tie to geography completely. The initial setup cost for an Internet store runs in the millions, yet one store can serve any connected consumer in the world. The fixed cost of setting up an Internet operation is very high, but the marginal cost of making the service available to more people is negligible.

4: **Cost of shelf space**. Traditional retailers are bound by the limits of shelf space. They can carry only as many different products as the store will hold. On-line businesses are not subject to this physical limitation because they do not hold in inventory much of what they offer for sale. Take, for example, the grocery business. A huge grocer, like Kroger, can stock about forty thousand items.[4] On-line grocers regularly offer over a hundred thousand items—in large part because they are distributing from a large central warehouse outside city limits and do not have to put all those items on retail shelves.

CONCLUSIONS

The competitive requirements of Dynamic Trade and the cost patterns associated with it—high fixed investments in intangible assets and extremely low marginal costs—suggest that Internet-based businesses will generate unprecedented economies of scale. However, these intangible assets do not offer an effective barrier to entry, and

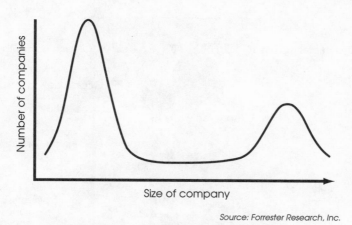

Size of company

Source: Forrester Research, Inc.

Figure 11   The Internet Supports Very Large and
Very Small Companies Best

therefore it is also likely that the Internet will support many very small players as well (see Figure 11).

Amazon and Barnes & Noble may dominate on-line book selling as they spend on technology and marketing. But the Internet makes the book business far more cost-effective for a little player, too. If, for example, a teacher wants to sell a few books to supplement her income, she can do it more cheaply on the Internet as an affiliate than she ever could by opening a bookstore or building a mail-order business. Therefore, it is likely that the Internet will support a thick cottage industry that acts as a wellspring of potential entrants (see Figure 12).

In this way, electronic commerce looks to me a bit like the software industry. In that market, there are only a few giant companies such as Microsoft, Oracle, and SAP. Economies of scale in distribution and technology development mean that large companies are far more profitable than smaller ones. Yet entry barriers remain low, and many new software companies form each year. Anyone with a good idea and a few programmers can revolutionize software. For the most part, the large players acquire or imitate smaller innovators. But because all the fixed assets of the largest player are intangible, their value can erode rapidly. Every few years, a big player such as Lotus or WordPerfect stumbles and gets acquired or replaced by an up-and-comer.

101

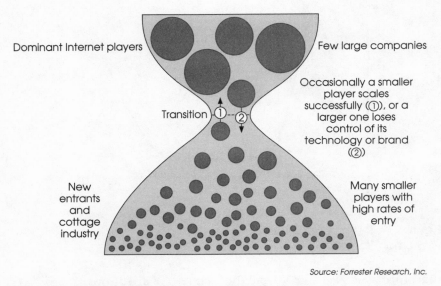

Dominant Internet players

Few large companies

Occasionally a smaller player scales successfully ((①)), or a larger one loses control of its technology or brand ((②))

Transition ①--②

New entrants and cottage industry

Many smaller players with high rates of entry

Source: Forrester Research, Inc.

Figure 12   Market Structure on the Internet

In Dynamic Trade, there will be no respite from competition, even for very large electronic commerce players. The cost economics of Dynamic Trade may ultimately result in there being fewer companies of a much larger scale than we saw before the Internet. Still, the rivalry among these companies and the ongoing threat of entry is likely to be very intense, especially around the struggle to gain control of key value creation points like consumer relationships, technology infrastructure, and sales distribution.

In the next chapter we'll look at how the Internet is changing the way companies earn revenues. With apparent supply driving down prices and the need to respond faster to current demand driving up costs, how does an Internet company make money? Chapter 7 will examine how Internet companies seize control of the business model in their industries by changing the revenue mix and putting traditional companies at a disadvantage as they try to respond. We'll look at how revenue mix is changing in three different industries and identify the patterns of attack that start-ups consistently employ when making a bid for the business of an incumbent.

CHAPTER 7

What Makes Internet Business Models So Difficult

As consumers shift their purchasing to the Internet, the business models that have defined traditional businesses for decades seem to be falling apart. Traditional company managers watch with increasing discomfort as new Internet competitors that have never earned a penny go public, rewarding their founders with millions—even billions—of dollars (see Figure 1).

Meanwhile, Internet companies are cutting prices to even below cost, and they are ratcheting up consumers' expectations for round-the-clock service and communication. At times, it seems as if the Internet will turn whole consumer industries into nonprofit ventures.

What is going on? In effect, the Internet is making it possible for new companies to dismantle the business models that define their industries and gain market share by doing so. Newcomers change the components of revenue and cost in such a way that traditional companies find it difficult to counterattack.

While the Internet's impact on business models varies from industry to industry, definite patterns have emerged. Taken as a whole, these patterns offer a valuable framework for thinking through how a company's financial performance will be affected by the transition to the Internet.

	Year founded	Year of IPO	Cumulative revenue 1996 to 1998	Two-year CAGR	Cumulative profit/ (loss) 1996 to 1998	Market capitalization June 1, 1999
AOL	1985	1992	$6,751	53%	($133)	$115,644
Amazon.com	1995	1997	$774	523%	($161)	$17,237
E*Trade	1982	1996	$544	88%	$1	$9,227
Onsale.com	1994	1997	$311[1]	281%	($17)	$361
Yahoo!	1994	1996	$295	208%	($6)	$28,563
Peapod	1989	1997	$154	58%	($44)	$160
Cyberian Outpost	1995	1998	$119[2]	181%	($34)	$247
CDNow	1994	1998	$80	199%	($56)	$334
Beyond.com	1994	1998	$54	149%	($38)	$704
eBay	1995	1998	$54[3]	989%	$3	$20,113
Priceline.com	1998	1999	$35[4]	n/a	($115)	$14,150
eToys	1996	1999	$25[5]	n/a	($17)	$5,523
Preview Travel	1985	1997	$23[6]	132%	($43)	$231

All numbers are in US$ millions.

1. Gross merchandise sales 1996 to 1998: $381 million, 176% two-year CAGR
2. Revenue and profit/loss data from March 1, 1996 to February 28, 1999
3. Gross merchandise sales 1996 to 1998: $848 million, 914% two-year CAGR
4. Revenue and profit/loss data from July 18, 1997 to December 31, 1998
5. Revenue and profit/loss data from October 1, 1997 to December 31, 1998
6. Gross bookings 1996 to 1998: $301 million, 214% two-year CAGR

Source: EDGAR Online, Inc.

Figure 1   Financial Data for Top Public Internet Companies

HOW INTERNET COMPANIES UNDERMINE TRADITIONAL REVENUE STREAMS

The hopeful dotcom company making its rounds to the venture capitalists in search of funding must create a business plan that is *inherently* tough for an established competitor to mimic. The fastest way to accomplish this goal is to undermine the pricing structure of the existing business. This strategy buys the dotcom time to grow. Existing players resist cutting prices, especially while electronic commerce still represents only a tiny fraction of total sales.

To attack the pricing structure of an industry, a start-up must realign all the components of revenues—in other words, it must change the *revenue mix* of an industry. Mix is simply *who* pays for *what*, and *how* (see Figure 2).

These three elements are highly interrelated. A start-up that wants to change the *how*, or pricing structure, must first find a way to alter *what* is being sold and also locate new customers—the *who*—to generate revenues to support the business.

- **Finding new customers.** In many cases, Internet companies will offer for cheap or free what traditional players sell, making up for the loss by developing new sources of revenue that didn't exist in the traditional business. For example, at Buy.com, advertising from corporate sponsors creates a revenue stream that supports lower prices on music, books, and electronics for consumers.

- **Offering new value.** Because the Internet lets companies gather and disseminate information more easily, it is often possible for an Internet company to create new value for consumers. For example, Internet auctioneer eBay offers value far beyond what traditional want ads do—even though both offer a way to buy and sell old furniture. On-line buyers see auctions as a new form of entertainment. They log in day after day, enjoying the action on items they are bidding for. For sellers, eBay has become an unofficial part-time job. Internet auctions play host to hundreds of specialized sellers who scour through catalogs, garage sales, and Goodwill stores, seeking items they think can fetch a high price at auction.

- **Building new pricing structures.** If an Internet challenger can identify new customers and offer new value, it can undercut the pricing of traditional players. But clever start-ups do more than just cut prices. They also repackage products so they can change *the way pricing is done* in an industry. eBay, for example, charges

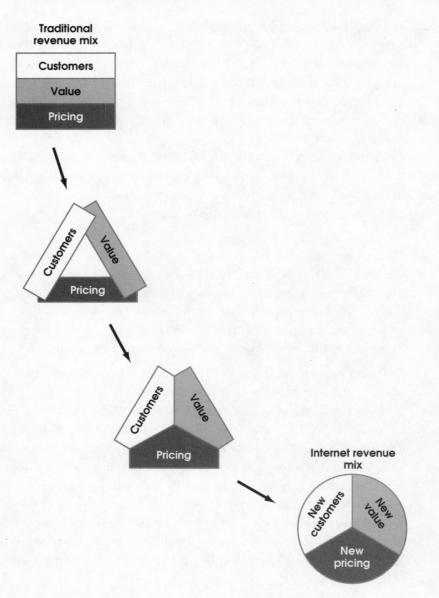

Source: Forrester Research, Inc.

Figure 2 Internet Companies Transform the Revenue Mix

sellers only a nominal amount for listing their product. Instead, it takes a percentage of the sale price. Traditional want ads usually charge much higher listing prices.

This three-pronged attack on the revenue streams that define an industry can be a potent weapon for newcomers. Traditional players find it extremely difficult to focus on new customers. This is particularly true of the strongest players, precisely because they are the businesses that have understood and served the existing customers of the industry well. Thus, traditional companies align their Internet efforts to their existing customers. Unfortunately, existing customers reflect an industry's past more than its future—they create a trap Forrester calls "the rearview mirror."

The rearview mirror can create very large distortions, as I discovered in a hotel suite in New York one afternoon. I had been asked to give a presentation about Internet trading to the executive team of a major brokerage house. So I outlined Forrester's projections for triple-digit growth in on-line brokerage. I told them that we expected an influx of new individual investors to the market and an eightfold to tenfold price decline in commissions. Suddenly, the leader of the group leapt to his feet and nearly shouted, "You're wrong! Investors want to talk to their broker on the phone! We've asked them, and that's what they told us!" He ran to the front of the room, grabbed my marker, and drew an X through the figure I had just drawn on the flip chart.

Fortunately, at that point, he realized that he'd better calm down—and he did. His reaction was more energetic than most, but his gut-level response is not atypical. Being a market leader makes it hard to see new customers coming. Unfortunately for this manager's company, it turned out that he was wrong about what new individual investors would want from brokers. In the months since his outburst, Internet trading has skyrocketed. Looking in the rearview mirror delayed the company's decision to build an Internet site by more than two years.

Understanding the new value offered by Internet companies is also hard for traditional players. In my experience, the reason for this myopia is that companies typically analyze a new challenger by comparing its products with what they already offer. In the memorable assessment of one executive from a regional telephone company, Yahoo! "is no different from the damn yellow pages, only nothing you really want is in there. People want to find local businesses."

Hardest of all for the traditional companies is the challenge of matching the prices offered by Internet start-ups. No one can poke fun at established companies on this count—the simple truth is that equity investors hold traditional players to a higher profit standard than they do the dotcoms. Moreover, traditional companies run strong, viable, valuable off-line businesses that would crumble if they were to match the on-line prices of Internet competitors willing to lose fifty cents on every dollar of sales. Such is the nature of competition in the United States that superliquid venture funds and individual investors can bankroll years of gigantic losses in a bid to win market share from traditional companies. As long as the dotcoms don't harm consumers—and lower prices hardly could—no one objects.

The net result, however, is that as more and more consumers move to the Internet, traditional companies are losing control of their revenue streams. To see how this is working in the real day-to-day competition of the Internet, let's look at what is happening in the markets for classified advertising, leisure travel, and financial services.

CLASSIFIED ADVERTISING WARS

Newspaper owners first saw how really destructive the Internet could be for their businesses in mid-1998. At about that time, I got a call from the owner of a daily paper in a midsized city. This man had been running the newspaper for more than a decade—the same paper his grandfather had founded before the turn of the last century. He wanted to come in to Forrester for the day to think through his response options to the threat of on-line classified advertising.

Before I tell you more about this client, let me describe the competitive situation he faced (see Figure 3). On the surface, every-

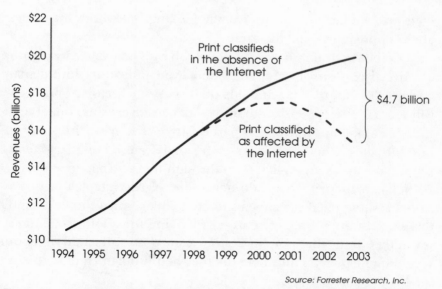

Source: Forrester Research, Inc.

Figure 3 The Effect of Internet Advertising on Newspaper Revenues

thing was fine. The newspaper had a stable readership and a near-monopoly position in its local market. The high cost of printing and delivering the paper ensured that there was only one other player in the city. Revenues consisted principally of subscriptions and classified advertisement for jobs, homes, and cars. The problem was that Internet start-ups had begun to offer classified listings on a national basis—focusing on just one of the big three categories. In the newspaper industry, these new Internet competitors came to be called category killers.

Let's look at how category killers are changing the revenue mix for classifieds. In the jobs market, newspapers' customers are local job seekers and corporate recruiters that advertise in the weekly and the Sunday supplement. On-line category killers like Monster.com and CareerMosiac, however, are finding *new customers*. They're not limited to local job seekers because they have a national reach—they can afford to since they don't have to print paper and deliver it. Not only that, but Internet companies reach non–job seekers. By letting people post their résumés in a database, the sites attract cov-

109

eted professionals who aren't really looking but who want to hear about opportunities all the same.

On the recruitment side, national job sites cultivate a new group of advertisers—small companies and even individual hiring managers, who find that placing ads on-line is much easier and, as we will see, far less expensive, than newspaper advertising. Small technology companies have been particularly active advertisers for on-line job sites. They find it far easier to isolate technology-literate potential employees on-line than through the newspaper.

Job category sites also add new value for recruiters. The professional résumé database appeals to companies, since the best candidates are often people who are not looking for a job. In addition, recruiters find that, on-line, they can post information about recruitment policies and benefits that help inform candidates and qualify prospects.

In the market for executive recruitment, FutureStep, an Internet business owned by Korn-Ferry and *The Wall Street Journal,* reaches midlevel managers who previously could not be reached cost-effectively through expensive face-to-face executive recruiters. Michael Bamberger, CEO of Korn-Ferry, describes this new opportunity: "Our clients complain that search firms have abdicated the middle market. The Net is a great way to efficiently serve it. By connecting the Internet with recruiters in our branch offices, FutureStep allows us to do this."

Essentially, the category killers opened up the market and undercut the newspapers' *pricing.* For the price of a single full-page ad in a newspaper like the *Boston Globe*—about $40,000—a company can place ten ads of four thousand words each for a month at a site like CareerMosaic, which reaches more than three hundred thousand unique visitors a day.

In the homes market, the pricing situation doesn't look much better. In fact, it's worse. Our newspaper owner typically took ads from real estate brokers, charging the same per-line fee he did for the job ads. It soon became apparent to the Realtors, however, that they could list homes for free at sites such as Realtor.com, owned by Homestore.com, the on-line listing service that represents the

National Association of Realtors. In addition, the multiple-listing service, which aggregates all the homes for sale nationwide, actually *sold listings* to Microsoft's Home Advisor Web site for a dollar per home.

Since listings provide no revenue stream, sites like Realtor.com and Home Advisor have built revenues around *new customers*, national advertisers that want to reach home buyers, including mortgage originators, moving companies, furniture makers, and telecommunications suppliers. To attract these advertisers, a site like Home Advisor had to develop a large audience. So Microsoft offered consumers new value. The site not only carries home listings but also helps consumers all the way through the home-buying process. Consumers can look up information about prospective schools, town leash laws, and local events. Once they find a home, Home Advisor will help them locate the cheapest mortgage on-line.

What about cars? Same story. Category killers like AutoWeb and Auto-by-Tel charge little or nothing for listing cars. Instead, they charge a fee when the dealer actually sells a car from a lead they generate. Consumers get auto reviews by authorities and other consumers as well as access to information on blue-book values, manufacturers' suggested prices, and recalls. Most of all, consumers like saying what car they want and getting a list of dealers that sell it.

Add it all up, and the competitive dynamics do not look good for our owner of a local newspaper. In fact, when Forrester interviewed recruiters, Realtors, and car dealers who had tried advertising on-line, they all said they planned to allocate more of the their budgets to the Internet and less to newspapers (see Figure 4).

One reason behind this shifting preference is the fact that on-line ads can be more complete than those in the newspaper. In addition, advertisers like being able to place perpetual ads—after all, recruiters, car dealers, and Realtors are continuously in the marketplace.

Beyond this, the advertisers told us that category killers offered them faster results at lower cost than newspapers ever had. A recruiter we interviewed said, "The Web improves our cycle time. One candidate told us that we made an offer before other firms had even acknowledged receiving a résumé. We can process résumés within one day and have them on a manager's desktop the next

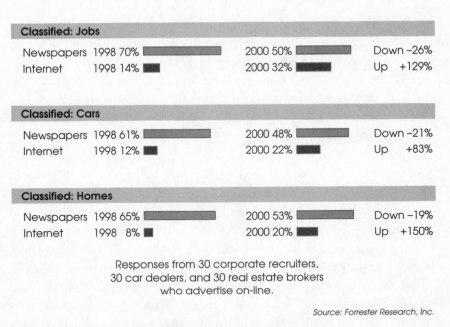

Responses from 30 corporate recruiters,
30 car dealers, and 30 real estate brokers
who advertise on-line.

Source: Forrester Research, Inc.

Figure 4 Allocation of Classified Advertising Budgets

day." On the subject of saving money, another commented, "In two years, we have received 140,000 résumés via the Web, made 1,900 offers, and 1,600 hires. Hires run at a cost of $10,000 in print—that's $16 million in savings."

One factor that helps this newspaper owner, at least temporarily, is the paper's consumer Technographics profile. More than half the newspaper's readers are technology pessimists, and anyway, consumers over thirty don't tend to use the Internet for news very much. Younger people do, in alarming numbers—and this will become a significant problem about five years from now. Moreover, the longer people are on-line, the more likely they are to prefer on-line over the paper as a medium for classifieds (see Figure 5).

During our meeting, we discussed three ways he could respond to the threat of the category killers. First, he could invest in the Internet companies that were attacking his core business and, in effect, join them as a minority investor. To the proud son of an old newspaper family, which had controlled the business utterly for over

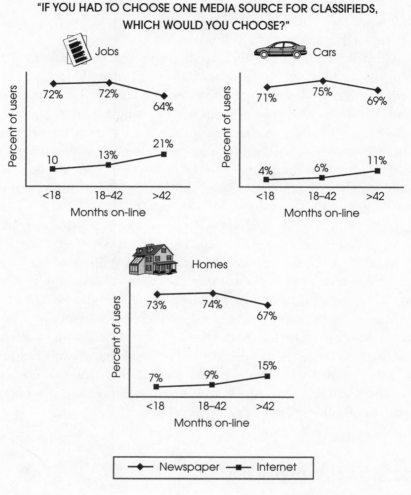

"IF YOU HAD TO CHOOSE ONE MEDIA SOURCE FOR CLASSIFIEDS, WHICH WOULD YOU CHOOSE?"

Source: Forrester Research, Inc.

Figure 5 Consumers with More On-line Experience Seek the Internet for Classifieds

a century, this felt like a failure—an admission that he couldn't run the business as well as his father and his grandfather before him.

Second, the owner could develop a local Web site to compete with the national category killers. This sounded more in keeping with the company's heritage, but the cost of developing a Web site as good as the category killers' sites would put the newspaper in a loss position for at least the next three years. And since many of his readers would continue to rely solely on the newspaper, he could not very well cut costs to fund the Web site.

Third, he could think about selling the newspaper rather than preside over its long, slow decline. After all, readership had been slowly falling for years, and Forrester's research with sixteen- to twenty-two-year-olds suggests it will not be rising anytime soon. And a direct hit on the classified business would hurt a lot because, although classifieds account for half the paper's revenue, they generate nearly all of the profit. Even a 10 percent price decline as a result of new Internet competition would mean confronting unionized workers with pay cuts and possibly layoffs.

In the end, the newspaper owner chose to develop his own Web site to compete head-on with the category killers. This choice felt, for him, most consistent with the stature and culture of the company. He also believes that most of his readers will continue to need the daily paper and that the local advertisers he has known for years won't soon defect. From my perspective, the choice he made is risky. I question whether he'll have the will to invest the millions of dollars running a state-of-the-art Web site in his local market will require. But more than that, I believe that even though his readers and advertisers will still do business with him, price pressure is going to shrink the traditional classified business.

TRAVEL AGENTS UNDER FIRE

The details of the challenges faced by the local newspaper owner are so specific to his industry that, at first glance, it may appear that his situation is unique. Yet similar dynamics exist in the travel business, even though the players, and the outcomes, are quite different. Three main groups vie for the attention—and dollars—of leisure travelers: travel suppliers such as airlines and hotels, traditional travel agents, and new on-line agents such as Travelocity, Priceline, Preview Travel, and Expedia.

Before the Internet, travel suppliers took four-fifths of their bookings through traditional travel agents and paid these agencies

114

7 percent of sales in commissions. Traditional travel agencies were highly fragmented, small companies—there were 30,300 of them in 1997.[1] This industry structure reflected the fact that most consumers booked leisure travel in Main Street stores, where they could sit down with an agent and review brochures.

Early in the battle for Internet consumers, the start-ups got the upper hand. Companies like Preview and Travelocity figured they could consolidate many more consumers on-line than any agency could from a single location. Major agency chains like Carlson Wagonlit and Thomson Travel incurred high costs setting up shops in every town and village where they did business. The start-ups didn't need to do that; they could direct all consumers to one Internet address. Internet companies also added new value for consumers in the form of travel content and tips. And they decided early on to take direct advertising from new customers such as hotels and tour operators to supplement their commission income.

It was not the start-ups that changed the pricing structure of the industry; travel suppliers did that. Airlines calculated that taking a booking on-line cost only between $12 and $15 a ticket, yet they were paying agents $30 for the average flight booking. If the airlines could sell directly to consumers, they could save the difference. So airlines announced to the world that they would cut commissions to traditional travel agents in half. More quietly, they told the major on-line agents that they would pay a flat fee—$10 a ticket—for bookings.

Shortly after that happened, I met with Terry Jones, president of Travelocity, to discuss the development. "The airlines are hurting us," he said. "They can't even book a ticket that cheaply themselves. How do they expect us to do it and make a profit?" Of course, they didn't. In fact, the last thing airlines want is on-line travel agencies. While airlines publicly praise their agents, in reality, airline executives wonder whether agents provide any value to them beyond physical presence. If the airlines could drive on-line agents out of the business and use only the Internet for direct bookings, so much the better.

In retrospect, I believe that one reason the first wave of Internet travel start-ups has struggled so much is that they did not seize control of the industry's pricing structure. Because commissions were

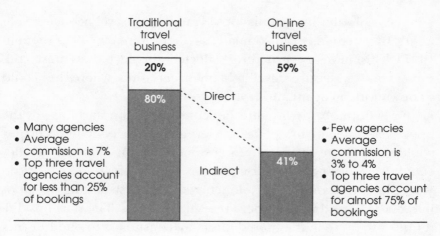

Source: Forrester Research, Inc.

Figure 6 The Impact of the Internet on the Travel Industry

cut to below cost, on-line agents' losses accelerated with every ticket they booked. All of them had significant financial backing, but who could thrive in this situation?

Then along came another Internet entrant, Priceline.com. Priceline put together all the elements of a new revenue mix: Consumers offer to travel when and where they desire, for a price they name. Airlines, desperate to keep 747s' seats full, fill the orders from excess inventory. Consumers pay a fee, but only if their order is filled.

Priceline shook up the industry when it entered the on-line market in 1998. And at first, airlines were as eager to chase Priceline away as they had been to halt the progress of the other on-line agents. Many airlines announced that they would not participate in the bidding system. In essence, airline executives feared entering a world of pure price competition. But soon many suppliers relented—though some of the larger ones, including United, American, and US Air, still avoid Priceline. In the end, though, it is just so expensive to fly an airplane with empty seats that it makes no sense to stay away from a Web site full of consumers offering to pay and fly.

As I write, direct bookings are the fastest-growing segment on-line—just as airlines had hoped. In fact, direct sales account for nearly 60 percent of Internet travel (see Figure 6).

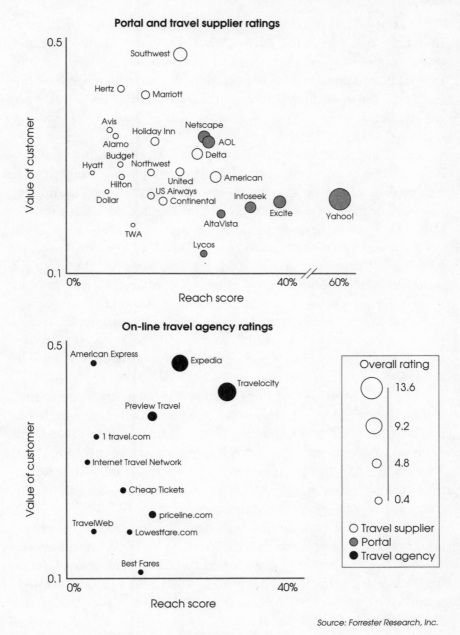

Figure 7 How Leading Travel Sites Shake Out

Source: Forrester Research, Inc.

Yet the suppliers' efforts to put the Internet start-ups out of business have not succeeded either. When Forrester graded Internet travel suppliers along three metrics—their reach, or traffic levels; their ability to motivate site visitors to book rather than just look online; and the spending power of the consumers they attract—we found that Travelocity and its partner Yahoo! have developed the top travel sites (see Figure 7).

Priceline occupies a unique position as an auctioneer of distressed airline inventory, and it has sought a patent on its pricing mechanism. However, Cheaptickets, which uses a more traditional discount pricing model and maintains friendlier relations with the airlines as a result, actually liquidates more unsold seats.

Expedia, Travelocity, and Preview Travel all continue to grow bookings—Travelocity alone sold $300 million in the first six months of 1999—and have developed secondary revenue sources from advertising. In addition, as more mainstream consumers come on-line, Internet agents are selling more profitable vacation packages that include car rentals and hotels. Together, the big on-line agents already rival the largest traditional agency chains in bookings.

The great irony is that low commissions have slowed entry into the on-line travel agency business. As a result, when on-line bookings grow to over $29 billion in 2003, existing on-line players will gain far more market power than traditional agents ever had. Enough, perhaps, to push commissions back up. In trying to stop the start-ups, travel suppliers may have sowed the seeds of a future travel agency oligopoly on the Internet.

What about the traditional agencies? The Internet has not been kind to them. Commission cuts forced many to begin charging consumers. But more telling is the rate of exit. The number of active traditional agencies fell 5 percent in 1998 and will fall as much again in 1999.[2] In mid-1999, only half of the top fifty traditional travel agents were able to take a consumer airline booking via the Web.

RESTRUCTURING THE BROKERAGE BUSINESS

Few industries have been as radically affected by new business models as the financial-services industry. If I had to pick a moment when the changes that have roiled the brokerage industry became inevitable, it would be that day all the way back in 1996 when E*TRADE announced that it would go public. Before that, the brokerage business had operated on a commission basis—with investors paying full-service brokers between 1 percent and 4 percent of the value of a trade, based on the size of the trade. Discount brokers such as Charles Schwab charged lower commissions but did not give investment advice as full-service brokers did. E*TRADE, however, charged a flat $29.99 per trade—and Internet brokerage took off.

It wasn't that E*TRADE was the first company to offer on-line trading—a company called K. Aufhauser, now owned by AmeriTrade, had done that back in 1995. Nor was it purely the pricing E*TRADE offered. Telephone discounters like Jack White and Patriot Brokerage were already fishing for individual investors with low prices—$17.76 per trade in the case of Patriot. What made E*TRADE matter so much was that it was well funded, with a $400 million investment from Softbank. This enabled E*TRADE to advertise widely. When the company offered its own stock to the public, it created a lot of buzz on Wall Street.

E*TRADE attacked the revenue mix of the brokerage industry. The company found new customers among individual investors who had not been active traders before. While these were not, strictly speaking, people new to investing, their activity volume rose considerably over what it had been in the traditional business. In the traditional model, small investors couldn't afford to trade much because their assets were so modest that trading commissions ate up any profit they made. E*TRADE also generated revenues from the investment banks that make markets in publicly traded stock. Market makers paid brokers for directing trading volume, or order flow, toward them.

However, it would not be long before a traditional player, Charles Schwab, took the lead in the on-line market. Schwab had launched on-line trading through a separate business unit called e.Schwab, at almost the same time as E*TRADE. While observers may have seen Schwab's move as a response to E*TRADE, Dave Pottruck, co-CEO of Schwab, says this wasn't so. "Our great fear at the time was that Intuit would enter the discount brokerage business. Intuit had six or eight million customers with Quicken, and together with Microsoft, they planned to offer on-line trading.[3] We had some discussions with them about delivering brokerage services, but they went their own way and we went ours. We expected to see them in the market, but we never did."

e.Schwab initially charged $39 a trade, figuring that it had the leading discount brand and thus would form a price ceiling for the industry. Pottruck says, "We understood our power. Whatever we charged, most of the industry would fall beneath us. So we never matched E*TRADE's, or anyone else's pricing." e.Schwab did eventually cut prices to $29.95, but not until E*TRADE was at $19.95 and others were trading as low as $10.

The e.Schwab business took off in 1997, with on-line assets swelling to $81 billion by the end of 1997 (see Figure 8).[4] However, Schwab increasingly found itself in a difficult position with respect the rest of the industry. As Pottruck describes it, "Despite our success, we found ourselves positioned in the press as the stuffy leaders, with the new companies as the challengers. The press loves the underdogs, so it was a difficult communication challenge that we had."

In addition, e.Schwab and Schwab were still essentially separate businesses. This caused confusion and some consternation among customers. The traditional brokerage, Schwab, offered on-line trading at a 20 percent discount to regular commission rates. So, telephone customers paid an average of $80 a trade, while Schwab Online customers paid $64 and e.Schwab traders paid $29.95. But if an e.Schwab customer wanted to talk to someone on the telephone, it cost $5 a call.

Going into 1998, Schwab changed its approach. It merged e.Schwab with Schwab and adopted a single rate scale for all its customers. But it wasn't pricing consistency that really mattered about the merger. It was a strategic shift. "We needed a way to get above

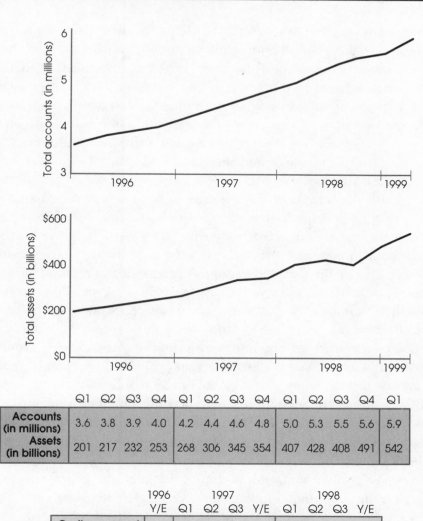

	Q1	Q2	Q3	Q4	Q1	Q2	Q3	Q4	Q1	Q2	Q3	Q4	Q1
Accounts (in millions)	3.6	3.8	3.9	4.0	4.2	4.4	4.6	4.8	5.0	5.3	5.5	5.6	5.9
Assets (in billions)	201	217	232	253	268	306	345	354	407	428	408	491	542

		1996 Y/E	1997 Q1	Q2	Q3	Y/E	1998 Q1	Q2	Q3	Y/E
	On-line percent of daily trades	25%	33%	36%	39%	37%	48%	52%	54%	54%
On-line activity	On-line accounts (in millions)					1.6				2.5
	On-line assets (in billions)					$112				$219

Source: Forrester Research, Inc.

Figure 8   Growth of Accounts and Assets at Schwab

121

bare-bones trading," says Pottruck. "Being the on-line firm with a little service wasn't good enough. We realized that what we really had to do was reinvent the full-service brokerage business. With the Internet, we found we had the means to deliver a lot better service to the individual investor in a tremendously cost-efficient way." Schwab set about to create a new segment in the brokerage business—a segment Forrester calls the midtier broker. Midtier brokers offer most of the advice and service provided by a full-service broker, at a fraction of the cost.

Until the advent of the Internet, individual investors basically fell into two camps. Delegators looked to full-service brokers like Merrill Lynch to advise them on investments and help them manage their money. Self-directed investors, of which there were many fewer, choose their own investment strategy. But in reality, many of the so-called Delegators were individuals who took an active interest in their investments—but still wanted advice. Schwab defined for itself a new category, the Validators—people who essentially manage their own money but who want verification of their strategies from a trusted source. The Validators, who would come mainly from among the customers of traditional full-service brokers, became the new customers of Schwab's move to become a midtier broker.

The Validators are on the whole a more mainstream customer target than the early adopters who first traded on-line in 1996 and 1997—including high-income pessimists as well as affluent optimists. To attract them, Schwab found that it had to change its message from one that emphasized using technology to one that focused on the customer's whole experience with Schwab. "We realized that we had to demystify on-line investing for the new customers coming on-line." To this end, Schwab focused its television and press advertising on "real people"—a message that resonated with people who did not think of themselves as technophiles.

New value comes mainly from the advice that Schwab offers to its on-line customers. This value extends well beyond the provision of research analysts' reports on-line and access to market and share information—which now even the lowest-price on-line brokers offer. Schwab's on-line advice is designed to help investors faced

SCHWAB'S DAILY STOCK PRICE SEP 1997–AUG 1999

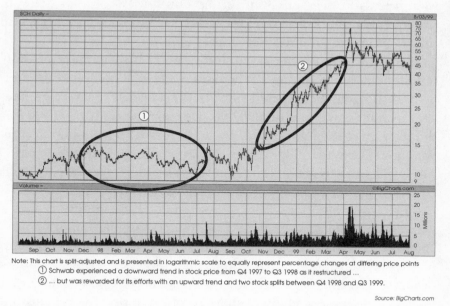

Note: This chart is split-adjusted and is presented in logarithmic scale to equally represent percentage changes at differing price points
① Schwab experienced a downward trend in stock price from Q4 1997 to Q3 1998 as it restructured ...
② ... but was rewarded for its efforts with an upward trend and two stock splits between Q4 1998 and Q3 1999.

Source: BigCharts.com

Figure 9   Schwab Weathers the Transition to Midtier Broker

with extreme choice. At OneSource, the company's mutual fund superstore, for example, customers can enter some characteristics they seek in a mutual fund, and the Web site will winnow the choices from hundreds to just a few. *New value* also comes from the flexibility that multichannel presence allows. Unlike E*TRADE customers, Schwab's can do business on-line, in one of Schwab's bricks-and-mortar stores, or over the telephone.

The merger of Schwab and e.Schwab took a significant short-term toll on the revenues and profits of the company. And, for the first two quarters of 1998, Schwab's stock was punished in the market (see Figure 9).

Going in, Pottruck had estimated that giving all of Schwab's customers access to $29.95 trading would reduce revenue by about $125 million. "We had models that showed how we thought we were going to make up that revenue. But to say that we had a *clear* idea of how is an excessive estimate of our foresight." The company believed that it would take two to three years to make up on volume

123

what it lost in price cuts. As it turned out, however, it took Schwab just fourteen months—from January of 1998 to March of 1999—to fully recover from the revenue impact of its move.

Schwab made up the revenue difference on volume. Not only did the number of accounts at Schwab rise from 4 million at the end of 1997 to 6.5 million by mid-1999, but the average assets in on-line accounts at Schwab rose to $90,000. This compares with $25,000 for the rest of the on-line brokerage industry. By aiming at the Validators, Schwab tapped into a more affluent customer base. These balances create additional revenue for Schwab in the form of float—the use Schwab has of its customers' money in the three days between when they buy a stock and when the trade settles.

Midtier players like Schwab, Fidelity, and Vanguard offer reasonably priced trading along with a lot of service, including account management, retirement planning, multiple channels for communication, and mutual fund choices. These players now form a distinct layer above competitors such as AmeriTrade, which focus on rock-bottom trading prices. E*TRADE falls in between—but is heading up-market toward the midtier as fast as it can.

As I write, full-service brokers such as Merrill Lynch and PaineWebber are just entering the on-line marketplace. They have resisted in large part because they employ thousands of highly paid brokers—who make their money on transaction fees that are many times higher than what midtier brokers now charge. Because full-service brokers do have strong relationships with very high-income clients, full-service brokers will do fairly well on-line, once they get going.

However, Forrester believes that the market shares in on-line brokerage will be vastly different from what they were in the traditional business. Full-service brokers held 85 percent of the traditional business, but Forrester expects them to account for just 22 percent of on-line accounts and 45 percent of assets in 2003 (Figure 10).

Midtier companies will focus less on pure trading and more on bringing together all of an individual's financial information and making it easy to use. That is the main reason Forrester expects the midtier to do so well.

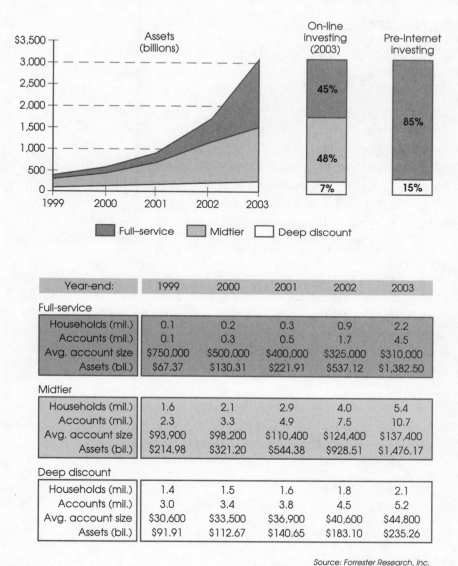

Figure 10 The Growth of On-line Investing

Year-end:	1999	2000	2001	2002	2003
Full-service					
Households (mil.)	0.1	0.2	0.3	0.9	2.2
Accounts (mil.)	0.1	0.3	0.5	1.7	4.5
Avg. account size	$750,000	$500,000	$400,000	$325,000	$310,000
Assets (bil.)	$67.37	$130.31	$221.91	$537.12	$1,382.50
Midtier					
Households (mil.)	1.6	2.1	2.9	4.0	5.4
Accounts (mil.)	2.3	3.3	4.9	7.5	10.7
Avg. account size	$93,900	$98,200	$110,400	$124,400	$137,400
Assets (bil.)	$214.98	$321.20	$544.38	$928.51	$1,476.17
Deep discount					
Households (mil.)	1.4	1.5	1.6	1.8	2.1
Accounts (mil.)	3.0	3.4	3.8	4.5	5.2
Avg. account size	$30,600	$33,500	$36,900	$40,600	$44,800
Assets (bil.)	$91.91	$112.67	$140.65	$183.10	$235.26

Source: Forrester Research, Inc.

CONCLUSIONS

The conclusion to be drawn from these three case studies—and in my experience, it is true in other industries as well—is that Internet start-ups follow consistent patterns of attack on traditional companies. They focus on *new customers, new value,* and *new pricing structures.* Changing all three at once makes it possible to undercut the prevailing revenue model.

While the start-ups usually open the attack on an industry's revenue model, the stories in this chapter clearly show that the ultimate winners and losers come from both camps. It can be tempting to see the battle of the Internet in black and white—start-ups versus traditional companies—and to conclude that one or the other is inherently better.

It is more realistic to say that the company or companies that define the on-line revenue mix do best in the Internet economy. Looking at the three cases above, the winners include newcomers, such as the classified category killers and on-line travel agents, as well as traditional players, such as airlines. The leading midtier brokers include Schwab, Fidelity, and Vanguard, as well as upstart E*TRADE. The other factor at work in all the success stories is scale. Internet businesses that bring together all the information, products, and customers in their particular niche do better than the ones that are limited to a single geography, product set, or group of customers.

In the following chapter we'll look at how companies that have established a lead can build a defensible strategic position amid the hot competition of the Internet. We'll focus on three strategies: developing a brand based on interactive experiences with consumers, building control over physical distribution, and leveraging consumer demand information.

CHAPTER 8

Creating Company Value

The early Internet is overrun with nearly identical companies. Exactly what is the difference between new superstores like Buy.com and ValueAmerica.com? Most consumers couldn't say. Internet companies seem to move in a pack, rushing from one hot idea to the next. First it was push technology, then one-click ordering. As I write, the hot spot is auctions. This "innovation," pioneered by eBay and Onsale, took Amazon and Yahoo! less than six months to copy. The point is that, in this environment, the strategy of one company is barely distinguishable from the strategy of any other.

The goal, then, for a company that intends to win in the long run is to head in a direction that may seem counterintuitive but that really allows it to build a uniqueness that is hard to copy. This chapter explores three paths to creating sustainable value in electronic commerce:

1. Develop a brand based on consumer experiences.
2. Control physical distribution.
3. Leverage consumer information.

DEVELOP A BRAND BASED ON CONSUMER EXPERIENCES

In our century of mass production, branding has been perhaps the most powerful means of separating a product from scores of undifferentiated suppliers. In fact, the less differentiated products actually are, the more important brand identity becomes.

Everyone can name a near-commodity product that gets a higher price because it has been branded. My favorite is Frank Purdue's chicken parts. If there is any product more blandly the same from one refrigerator package to the next, I can't name it. Yet Frank Purdue has managed to persuade me and millions of other consumers that we should trust him more than anyone else to turn out a decent chicken in every package.

Purdue accomplished branding superiority with his own image as a tough businessman who cared about nothing but winning the chicken sale. As a consumer, you had the sense that he would boot out of his company any person who dared to doubt the importance of chicken parts, and that Frank would personally eliminate any chicken that couldn't cut it as a Purdue. And as long the chicken itself was no different—that is, no worse—than any other you'd ever had, you had to figure that Purdue's chickens were as good as the best.

This basic aspect of consumer brands—that the experience of the product itself is in some ways secondary to the image or associations of the brand—creates both a challenge and an opportunity on the Internet. The challenge is that the Internet will not allow a one-way presentation of the brand *image*, as television and print advertising do. Instead, with electronic commerce, the brand emerges as the sum of two-way communication *experiences* that the consumer has on-line (see Figure 1).

The opportunity is that a brand built on two-way experiences is far more powerful and lasting than any projected image. Think of this experiential branding as a kind of bridge between consumers and a company. This bridge is built of hundreds of individual experiences that gradually weave together to form a stronger and stronger bond between the two. Over time, each consumer accumulates so many experiences that he or she forms a set of deeply held beliefs about the brand. Once that happens, the consumer tends to reject a negative experience as an exception unless the negative experiences become too numerous or overwhelming to ignore.

	Image	Experience
Interaction	One-way	Two-way
Communication	Personality	Dialogue
Content	Constant	Cumulative
Development	Created by an agency or marketing team	Evolves as a product of interaction
Delivery Medium	TV	Internet

Source: Forrester Research, Inc.

Figure 1 On the Internet Companies Must Build Brands Based on Experience

Experiential branding isn't new, and it doesn't require the Internet.[1] In fact, companies that have built experiential brands in the past have been able to do so *because* of their physical presence. Both McDonald's and Disney have executed the kind of experiential branding I am talking about. As consumers, we have all had scores of experiences at McDonald's where the restaurant was clean, the service fast, and the hamburger exactly as we expected it to be. If we do happen to encounter a McDonald's that fails to meet this standard, we recognize it as an exception.

Disney's experiential branding is even more remarkable. Now before I go on to praise Disney, I have to tell you that I am not a Mouse fan. I despise how Disney has homogenized classic fairy tales like Cinderella and Snow White, and I consider the Pocahontas movie a cultural hijacking. In our family, we joke about "the Disney Tax," the amount of money every American family pays to Disney each year to keep their kids quiet.

Despite this jaded outlook, my husband and I took our extended family on our first trip to Disney World last year. Over the course of a week, we had an extraordinary experience. It started the minute we got there. We arrived late and trudged off to the restaurant to eat. The waitress who served us dinner saw how tired we were. "These kids look beat. Do you want me to wrap up the dessert so you can take it back to your room?" she asked. Yes, we would! We hadn't even thought of that.

The next day, trying to get to the Buzz Lightyear ride, we got stuck with our two children, their three cousins, and my in-laws in a parade on Main Street USA. When I asked a nearby Disney employee for directions, he opened a door behind him, walked us right off the Main Street set, and led us across the back lot, where he opened another door and let us out in front of Buzz. "Have a great time," he said. We did!

I could go on and on . . . how the roller-coaster operator helped me and my daughter after one ride made her ill . . . how unbelievably accommodating the restaurants were as my British relatives ordered items that weren't even on the menu . . . how employees always kept the lines moving and provided a diversion while we waited. The point is that we had so many good experiences at Disney World, delivered with such resounding goodwill, that any mishap seemed like a fluke. Truly, the experience was "magical," just as Disney had promised. Nothing in a television advertisement could ever build the kind of brand associations that our trip to Disney World did.

It used to be that to create an experiential brand, you had to run a business that people could *visit*. That is why the best examples of consumer experience brands are theme parks, restaurants, and stores. But with the Internet, the possibility of creating an experiential brand is now open to any company that builds a Web site. How you respond to people who encounter your company on the Internet suddenly becomes far more important to your brand than what your advertising tells them.

The hard part about experiential branding, as anyone who is married can tell you, is that managing a two-way communication well over time is *tremendously* difficult. It is far more challenging than hiring the top creative talent to come up with great TV ads. The very nature of the network makes controlling the experiences a consumer has with your company and its products very challenging.

One of my clients, a personal-care products company, began struggling with this issue recently. The company has totally different brand images in the United States and Australia. In the United States, its family-oriented shampoo and soap brands bring to mind associations of motherhood and gentleness. In Australia, the company strikes a hip note, appealing mainly to teenagers. Not only that, but Australian culture permits—in fact, expects—more open and relaxed attitudes. So on its Australian site, the company featured humor about skin problems and straight talk about sex for teens.

The differences in the company's brand images in the United States and Australia presented no problem—until Americans began to visit the site down under. What was purely mainstream in Australian culture was shocking to the average conservative American. The experiences that Internet consumers have when they encounter the Australian site rapidly erode the "family life" image this company has so carefully cultivated in the United States.

The difficulty of building a brand based on consumers' Internet experiences is precisely what makes it such a powerful strategic asset. Very few companies will be able to do it well because experiential branding is not about a concept—it is all about dogged execution. The challenge is to create brand experiences that are consistent and reinforcing across five distinct areas:

- **On the Web site.** For a company that wants to create an experiential brand, its Web site is its single most valuable asset. As far as Internet consumers are concerned, the company *is* its Web site. The grace, speed, and effectiveness of the Web pages themselves will determine what consumers believe about your brand. And delivering a unique and memorable experience—one so closely associated with your company that no one can effectively copy it—is critical. This experience cannot be a process like one-click ordering or a bidding mechanism, for these processes, once copied, become so ubiquitous that no one can remember who created them. The early Internet offers few examples of

131

unique, branded experiences. Amazon and Yahoo! serve consumers well on their sites, and they have tremendously high name recognition, but these "brands" really don't carry any palpable associations. America Online, by contrast, has a distinctively "mainstream America" personality to it—accomplished in part by the audible phrase "You've Got Mail."

- **In the store**. So far, bricks-and-mortar retailers have been much slower than catalog merchants in creating effective links with consumers on-line. One glaring problem is the lack of consistency between on-line and off-line stores. In fact, when Forrester did a study of the top on-line apparel sellers in mid-1999, catalog merchants offered a median of ten thousand different items on-line—as many or more than they did in their catalogs. Internet-only start-ups offered twelve thousand, but bricks-and-mortar retailers listed only a thousand items for sale. In an environment where apparent supply is increasing, these retailers make themselves look lost.

- **Through personal communication**. When consumers order on-line, they wonder, Did they get my order? Is everything OK? Companies that build a good experience tend to overcommunicate, confirming orders, shipment, and billing by e-mail. Great companies go much further—they respond to *all* e-mail originating from the Web site and they coordinate telephone and e-mail service.

- **Over the Internet**. What comes up when your company's name is typed into AltaVista? How about Lycos? Do you know? You *must,* because the consumers' experience *begins* on those search sites. It's dangerous if your company either doesn't show up or shows up in a strange way, such as "XYZ to fire workers in labor dispute." Whether you plan for it or not, others will use your company's name, logo, products, and content to build their Web sites. But you cannot build an experiential brand unless you manage the company you keep on the Internet. It starts with simply knowing who links to your company, how your company performs on search sites, and who is selling your products and using your name. After that, you can begin to think about how and where consumers *should* experience your brand on the Web and then make it happen.

- **Off the Internet.** From a consumer's point of view, especially a mainstream consumer, the company you present on-line should be the same one they know off-line. The more coordinated the message, look and feel, and product offerings are between a company's off-line presence and its on-line one, the better. When consumers find a new site, such as The Knot, which offers wedding planning, they find it far more comfortable to return if their on-line experience is reinforced when they're off-line. The Knot recognized that early, and as a result, it promotes on the radio, in a magazine, and through books that its cofounder and etiquette expert, Carley Roney, has written.

CONTROL PHYSICAL DISTRIBUTION

In the end, there is nothing virtual about Internet businesses. Products that get sold on the Web have to be delivered. Every successful, fast, and accurate delivery creates a positive brand experience, just as each botched delivery job detracts from the brand.

On the early Internet, few companies seem to understand this. Entrepreneurs are so excited about the possibility of slapping together a company in thirty days or less that they ignore the physical realities of delivery. As an analyst, I encounter this fault in almost every one of the start-ups that march through Forrester on their public-relations blitzes. One of them, a Web-based health-care company that specializes in natural vitamin supplements, is a good example. "How will you handle delivery?" I asked the thirty-two-year-old CEO. "Oh, we've got a distribution company that'll do that for us. They pick the stuff, pack it, and ship via UPS or whatever." Whatever, indeed.

Superior physical delivery is going to be one of the most important strategic advantages that an Internet business can have. Almost anyone can take an order. But to process it well and to get the right product into the hands of the consumer *today*—not in three to five business days, as most Internet companies do now—will be rare. It seems inconceivable now, but in all likelihood, Internet retailers will guarantee that orders taken by noon will be delivered by five o'clock the same day. Companies will pick products from local warehouses and pack them within an hour of receiving an Internet order. Excellent product delivery will be a critical link in the brand experience for consumers on the Internet (see Figure 2).

Building a distribution network that gets everything from shoes to fresh fruit off the Internet and into consumers' homes isn't easy. Financing a truck fleet, training drivers to be reliable and polite, and operating a warehouse that deals with different products, some of which may require refrigeration, twenty-four hours a day, is hard. So hard, in fact, that only a few companies will be able to do it—con-

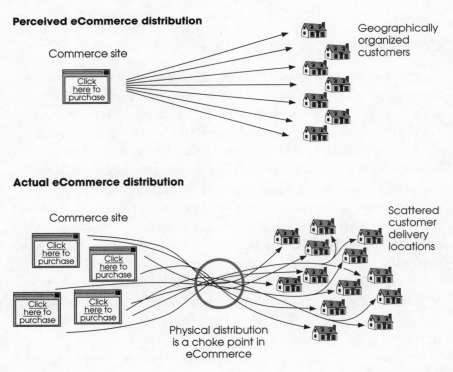

Source: Forrester Research, Inc.

Figure 2 Physical Distribution Reality

solidation into just a few players is likely. Those companies that succeed will tend to dominate their regions. This leads to several important implications:

- First, businesses that build physical to-the-home distribution channels will possess a highly profitable and defensible asset. Home delivery is a natural monopoly. It always makes sense to consolidate all home deliveries into one company because it reduces the cost for all parties. That is why newspapers that compete tooth and nail for editorial and classified ads in a town almost always put their rivalry aside in order to share the delivery routes.

  Internet grocery companies have made the biggest early investments in home delivery. As an example, considered the five-year-old company Streamline, which is based in the Boston area. Streamline takes orders over the Internet and then delivers groceries, videos, dry cleaning, and even stamps to homes. But the company has to sign up a high percentage of people on each street that its trucks run past in order to make a profit.

  Slowly, street by street, Streamline and others like it have been signing up homes and building the logistics infrastructure to deliver goods to them twice a week. Eventually, companies like Streamline could become the conduit to homes for a broad array of physical goods ordered on the Internet. This would put on-line grocers in a powerful position relative to consumer packaged goods suppliers like Procter & Gamble, which cannot sell over the Internet without such a distribution system.

- Second, direct marketers skilled in individual order management have a significant advantage over bricks-and-mortar retailers. Take the case of Lands' End. The company is in the middle of a turnaround following a period of weakness. The company's comeback is being driven in part by its move to the Internet. On-line, Lands' End has done very well—ringing up $61 million in product sales over the Web in 1998. As Bill Bass, VP of electronic commerce, told me, "There's no conflict for us the way there is for the retailers. The Internet is all good news—lower costs, more consumers, growth." The difference is that Lands' End, like other direct merchants, has already perfected a system of getting an individual order picked from the warehouse and packed for shipment within a day. In 1998 alone, Lands' End sold direct to over six million different households and shipped more than fifteen million packages that arrived on the doorstep just three to five business days after the order was placed.

- Third, retailers that can link Web orders with in-store stock will possess an advantage over Internet-only players that lack a physical presence. Most consumers would rather get their goods faster than in three to five days, which is how long typical Internet orders take to get delivered by mail. Traditional retailers such as Nordstrom already are beginning to capitalize on this advantage. They let consumers preshop on the Internet to see what Nordstrom carries before traveling to the store. If a consumer seeks an item they once saw in a Nordstrom mailer or a catalog, but cannot find that item on the Web site, they can send an e-mail to a Nordstrom Shopper, who will help them locate the product in one of Nordstrom's retail stores. Superstores and grocery stores can prepack large orders for consumers who want to save time on the basics but prefer to shop in person for special items.

- Fourth, distributors must adapt to home delivery. Big distribution companies like Ingram have excelled in getting goods from the manufacturer to the retail store. They now have a tremendous opportunity to develop the ability to pick and pack individual orders and to see the delivery through to the consumer, either via air shippers or through links to home- delivery systems like Streamline. Because of the economies of scale in warehouse operations, it is likely that only a few very strong distribution companies will remain.

- Finally, delivery companies like UPS, FedEx, and DHL are poised for growth in their home delivery business as more and more products are bought on-line. I have worked with executives at some of these companies, and it is clear that they see a major opportunity.

LEVERAGE CONSUMER INFORMATION

Every day, the Internet generates a mind-boggling amount of new data. Every log-on, every click, every Web site registration, and every e-mail creates a trace of data on a computer. But no one has figured out how to use this information. In 1996, I visited a company called IPro, which was then in the business of auditing the traffic on Web sites. The president at the time, Ariel Poler, took me in a back room to show me the kind of information the company was collecting. "Want to see Excite?" he asked. "Here it is, this is yesterday on Excite." I was looking at a pile of paper, a computer printout *several feet* thick. So what did IPro find? Nothing, at least nothing of any value, could be found in that huge stream of data.

That was over three years ago, and the traffic on Excite and other Web sites has since expanded a hundredfold. More data! More data! But for all the talk about the measurability of Internet commerce, very little progress has been made in *using* that data. In 1999, when Forrester conducted a study of Web sites, we asked managers what they do with all the information generated on their sites. The answer: mostly nothing.

It is notable that the most innovative idea about how to use the data on Web sites was generated in 1996 by a company founded by an artificial intelligence expert from MIT, Pattie Maes. That company, Firefly Networks, used the information about which music CDs customers bought to infer what other titles they might like. In 1999, this is still the single, tired example of using customer information to sell more—though the idea is now in use at Amazon, CDNow, and many other stores.

Why the information paralysis? The bottom line is that, on the Internet, getting data is very easy, but putting it to valuable use is not. In part, this is a technology problem—a lack of software programs to process Web data and cull useful conclusions from it. But even if such software were available, every site measures the data slightly differently. The situation is a bit like the one in old England, when height was measured in hands or feet, and weight was reckoned in stones. These measures were quite variable until Queen

Elizabeth I standardized them to inches and pounds. Similarly, Web sites collect "clicks," "page views," and "unique visits," but the definitions of those measures vary from site to site. The result is that very few Web sites are able to use the information they collect. A company that develops the ability to act quickly on data that it collects from the Internet will possess a hard-to-copy advantage.

Many companies hold back on developing that ability because they fear a consumer backlash over privacy. And this is an important concern, especially since lawmakers have not been able to keep pace with changes in consumer and business behavior around the Internet. No guidelines exist for what is appropriate, and no precedent defends a company's right to use any of the information it generates. In all likelihood, some unlucky company will soon become society's lab rat for the privacy issue. It will misuse data in a way that causes a massive consumer protest, then face legal action, finally causing the Supreme Court to review what constitutes an individual's personal information boundaries.

Waiting until society generates acceptable rules around information is a safe strategy. But it is better to forge ahead despite the uncertainty. To build a strategic advantage around using information, a company must act first—before it has permission. But in order to protect itself and its customers, it must take the high ground on the issue of privacy.

Taking the high ground means using information about demand in a way that helps consumers as a group and respects them as individuals. Most companies fail to do either one or the other because they end up mixing personal information with collective data. In fact, the two are quite distinct (see Figure 3).

- **Personal information.** Information such as addresses, names, credit-card numbers, and purchasing history must be used only to assist one particular consumer to make a faster, easier, and better decision about what he or she needs.
- **Collective data.** Information about the total demand for a given product or about the way demand responds to pricing changes contains less potential for privacy violations. Therefore, collective

	Personal information	Collective data
Description	Information about an individual	Aggregate totals for a population
Examples	Credit card number, address, gender, race	Total demand, price sensitivity of products, time of day of purchase
Acceptable uses	Product suggestions, one-click check out, faster, better service	Product promotions, price changes, identifying sales peaks
Risks to avoid	Discrimination, violation of privacy	Mixing personal information with collective data

Source: Forrester Research, Inc.

Figure 3   Appropriate Use of Personal Infomation and Collective Data

data can be used to adjust a company's pricing, product offerings, and target markets.

Since personal data is a most sensitive area, companies should only collect such information *explicitly*—in other words, by asking the consumer. Collective data can be gathered without the knowledge or consent of consumers. However, to steer clear of privacy concerns, the data must never link back to any particular consumer's personal information or to sensitive aggregates such as such as income, gender, and race.

Even aggregate personal information can lead to a fiasco, as Fleet Bank discovered. The bank observed that mortgage lending to African Americans was riskier on average, and so it began charging higher mortgage rates to blacks. Following complaints of customers, first the Federal Reserve Bank and then the U.S. Justice Department charged the company with discrimination. Fleet initially tried to defend itself—it claimed that it really charged higher rates to people with lower incomes and that these were disproportionately black.

At that point, the press and public turned such a critical eye toward the company that it settled quickly and apologized. The message from the public was clear. Fleet had no business tying collective data such as mortgage performance to personal information such as race—not even as an aggregate. Charging different rates for different types of loans is fine; charging higher rates for one type of person versus another is not.

Fleet's information nightmare didn't involve the Internet at all. In fact, these events happened in 1993–1994, on private computers.[2] Companies must be even more vigilant on the Internet because the fear of privacy violations already has been raised. To be safe, a company must not only avoid using personal information to generate market insights but must also be able to show that it actually has no means of doing so.

Companies should think of personal information and collective data as the church and state of Internet business. Keep the two separate.

With this rule about the separation of personal information from collective data, it becomes much easier to think about how a company can create a strategic advantage using information.

USE PERSONAL INFORMATION TO CREATE A BRAND EXPERIENCE

Using personal information well is the essence of delivering a great brand experience. Yet the experience can be created only with the cooperation of the consumer. After all, experiences are two-way events. Too much effort has gone into the idea of building a Web site that guesses what consumers want and surprises them with it. This kind of thinking has led to some very stilted efforts at creating personal experiences—starting with a personal greeting. Yet what could be less personal than entering a Web site that shouts, "HELLO, Mary Modahl" on its top line? This always makes me feel like shouting back, "Hello, stupid automated system."

Good use of personal information requires a far more subtle approach, where the consumer provides information in order to make his or her experience a better one. Take, for example, the ordering experience at the Clinique makeup site. Clinique has collected from me information about my skin type, eye color, and hair. In addition, the company has my credit-card information as well as shipping addresses for my home and office. Now when I go to Clinique, the company can offer me new makeup colors or skin-care products that are right for my type. When I check out, I can click on which shipping address I want for this order instead of reentering all that data. As a consumer, the experience is easier and better because Clinique has some information.

The information exchange between a company and a consumer is like a dance in which many small steps add up to a single, branded experience. There is a certain mystery to it—an art. But there is no deception. The consumer openly shares some information, and the company makes life easier for the consumer as a result.

Fingerhut, the mail-order catalog company described in chapter 5, has brought this dance to a high art. According to the company's president, Will Lansing, Fingerhut operates a nine-terabyte database containing customer records with up to 3,500 attributes per consumer. "People think we're just a junk-mail company," says Lansing. "But that's exactly what we're not. Our whole game is *not* sending people junk mail but sending them mail they clearly want." How does Fingerhut figure out what people want? "We gather behavioral data—what people actually buy from us over time. Then we match that individual consumer information against the attributes of our catalogs to determine which ones of the 135 different mailings we do in a year to send out to each customer."

Fingerhut treads carefully to avoid crossing the line between valuable information exchange and violated privacy. "We guard the data fiercely," says Lansing. "We sell it to no one, and we use personal information only with permission from our customers."

Companies that differentiate themselves by using personal information well must measure the effectiveness of their efforts by calculating how much revenue is created per consumer on the Web site. If you think of a consumer's stream of purchases today, tomorrow, next year, and so on for the lifetime of the consumer, how much can your company sell to this consumer? How much more would this consumer buy over that time if your company offered superior service based on personal information? A company that generates $150 a year per consumer is going to do far better than one that averages just $30.

Thinking about an Internet business as a stream of revenues from individual consumers also proves to be fairly helpful in a business environment where few companies earn a profit. How can you fairly value a business in such an environment? Clearly, the stock market has been having some trouble assigning a reliable value to Internet stocks. I believe that revenues generated per site visitor turns out to be one of the most stable measures anyone can use to gauge whether a company is actually creating value.

Take, as an example, my dad, the technology pessimist who buys at Amazon. How much is it worth to Amazon to have signed him up? Well, my dad buys about $500 worth of books in a year. If Amazon can so delight him that he spends half his annual book budget online in each of the next five years, my dad is worth something over $1,000, depending on how much value you assign to getting the money over five years rather than right away. But if my dad has to keep reentering credit-card numbers and addresses, and if the store doesn't keep track of personal information that makes doing business easy, my dad might spend just $100 a year on-line. In that case, he would be worth less than $500 to Amazon.

Naturally, you would have to subtract the cost of the books. But because many of the costs of running an Internet business are fixed, you might say that a company is really worth the value of its customers' spending streams over time minus the probable fixed costs. When you see a business this way, it becomes clear that, next to growing the actual number of customers, using personal information well to increase *sales per customer* is the fastest way to increase the value of an Internet business.

USE COLLECTIVE DEMAND DATA TO CHALLENGE OLD BUSINESS MODELS

While using personal data may improve the experience that consumers have doing business with you, trying to use personal information to gain marketwide insight can be dangerous for Internet businesses. Despite the exciting possibility of targeting consumers very narrowly—say, only people in one town, or only those who spent a certain amount on Visa last year—the potential sensitivity of consumers around privacy is so high that businesses run an unacceptable risk trying to do so.

Instead, companies should look for marketwide insights from collective demand data—data about products, prices, and time-of-day behavior. Initially, it may seem that this type of data is less interesting than personal information. But in fact, collective data can be very valuable in creating a kind of operational excellence that is tough to copy.

Web sites, for the most part, do not gather very good collective data, and those that do rarely use the information. But occasionally in our research at Forrester we turn up companies that really do a good job of it. These companies create a remarkable amount of value by using their collective data well. One company in particular comes to mind. I came across it as part of the research for a report on Web site performance. This company had gathered and mapped the sales made on its site against the speed at which the Web pages came up for consumers. During low traffic times, when the Web site was fastest, the company noticed that it sold more per page view than it did during peak load times, when the site ran more slowly.

The company was able to quantify the result of speeding up the performance of its site in dollar terms. It turned out that doubling the speed at which the Web pages loaded on the consumer's PC *more than doubled* the amount of money that the consumer would spend. But most important, this company acted very quickly on its collective information. It stripped out any unnecessary graphics and streamlined the site's design so it ran faster, especially for consumers with modem connections. And it added more computer and network capacity.

This example is compelling because the implications of the collective data were so clear and the company acted on the information. And the uses of collective data are in no way limited to Web site performance. In fact, I believe that collective data is most useful to companies that want to establish an advantage around a new business model because it lets a company rethink the revenue mix of its business. Companies can:

1: **Measure the price sensitivity of a product.** This is particularly important in markets where the number of potential buyers of a product appears to be growing, as is the case with individual investment, for example, and cellular telephones. In these markets, it is useful to know that if you dropped the price of the product in half, would the amount sold double, triple, or remain the same? On the Internet, companies can try out such daring moves far more easily. Not only is it simpler to change prices on a Web site than in stores and paper catalogs, but the results can be measured almost immediately.

2: **Address new customers.** Angela Kapp, vice president and general manager of Estée Lauder's on-line division, runs the Clinique makeup site I mentioned earlier in this chapter. Kapp says that one of the big surprises of the site was that it attracted so many people who had never done business with Clinique before. In fact, in the first six months, 20 percent of the buyers were new customers, and 40 percent of the orders included products that the consumer had never bought from Clinique before. Suddenly, it became apparent to Estée Lauder that the Web site, in addition to opening a channel to existing customers, could be used to create new relationships and test new products fast.

3: **Use time as an advantage.** Any frequent flier can tell you the peak demand for airline tickets in the United States is over

November's Thanksgiving week. In Europe, the top ski week of the year is the February school vacation. But this kind of timing insight is much less obvious when it comes to individual products. Toys sell best at Christmas—but how long does it take for the maker of a hot toy to find out that the demand is actually three times what it has projected? And how many more can the company make before the buzz about this hard-to-get toy fades? Generating this kind of accurate and to-the-minute demand data will be the main value of collective data. Seeing that baggy jeans have attracted teen tastes and slim-fit pants are "out," or spotting a trend toward green vehicles rather than silver ones, can help a company respond to its market faster.

CONCLUSIONS

As the Internet matures from a sideshow in consumer business to a major source of revenues, it will change the competitive dynamics of most consumer industries quite dramatically. Companies can expect mounting downward price pressure as apparent supply expands and more volatile prices as consumers come to expect companies to respond to them rather than the other way around.

To win in this environment, companies must quickly build a critical mass of customers and enough technology know-how to respond to current demand as it fluctuates. That means investing in intangible assets, particularly the sales distribution channels that will build the customer base and the technology that will respond to consumers.

To cover these costs, companies must build revenues as quickly as possible. Yet the Internet is enabling start-up companies to change the way revenues are earned in many industries. As a result, these start-ups are undercutting the pricing structures that traditional companies have come to take for granted. While it is most often Internet companies that attack the revenue models of an industry, an analysis of several different markets shows that this offensive position does not always guarantee victory. In fact, the companies that do best on the Internet are those that seize control of the revenue mix—*who* buys *what* and *how*. Either type of company can succeed at this strategy.

In the end, however, even building a business to scale quickly will not guarantee a company's ongoing success. The barriers to entry in Internet businesses are low, and most likely will remain so. Companies can expect to see a thick and constantly churning layer of entrants—from which every year one or two companies will break out and race up to scale. This pattern is typical of software, networking, and other computer- technology-based industries. In the Internet economy, all businesses are technology-based.

To combat this ongoing competitive environment, companies must create a defensible strategic position. That strategic position could be built around an experiential brand—one built from two-way interactions with consumers, control of physical distribution, or superior access to and ability to use information about consumer demand.

Any company, whether it be a venture-backed Internet start-up or a traditional company with a hundred years of history, has the opportunity to win the battle for Internet consumers. But traditional companies are at an undeniable disadvantage. Older companies struggle to free themselves from the history of how they have always done business. I call this the gravity factor—the pull that keeps a company from changing enough to compete effectively in the Internet economy.

In Part Three, we'll look at how traditional companies can defy the gravity that binds them to the past. We'll look at the challenge of managing technology change and why classical IT management won't work for the Internet. We'll consider the thorniest issue in all of electronic commerce: channel conflict. Manufacturers have long been partners with retailers and distributors, but now these partners are standing in the way of closer relationships with their consumers. Manufacturers must find a way to cut through this impediment or they will find themselves at a significant disadvantage in on-line selling. Finally, and not least, we'll look at the role of funding, organization, and leadership in driving success on the Internet.

PART 3

Defying the Gravity of the Old Ways of Doing Business

CHAPTER 9

Thriving on Technology Change

Every successful traditional company has, over the years, built up a set of shared experiences that inform its business practices and create a corporate mythology. These myths and traditions are fundamental to a company's identity. They are reflected in the way it serves its customers, how its meetings are held, and who makes decisions. In addition, established companies have sunk investments—in technology, distribution, and brand identity. For the most part, these assets have been costly to build and constitute a primary source of competitive advantage.

Yet the established ways of doing business also create a gravity field around a company's operations and even its thought processes. The gravity constantly pulls the company toward tradition—away from innovation and change, particularly changes that affect the revenue mix and customer relationships. Even well-managed companies can find it difficult to defy the gravity enough to compete effectively on-line. Since a company's established practices, key assets, and know-how are often the *source* of competitive differentiation in the first place, they can be hard to cut loose. Yet gravity is a dangerous liability in the new economy. By holding back traditional firms, it makes them far more vulnerable to the incursions of start-ups.

In Part Three of *Now or Never,* we will examine three major sources of gravity that established companies must manage. This chapter discusses how companies can thrive on technology change;

chapter 10 looks at how they can cope with channel conflict; and finally, chapter 11 looks at how to align funding, leadership, and organization for the Internet Economy.

We begin by looking at the gravity created by the investments and practices that traditional companies have built up around technology management. For most traditional companies, an investment in IT infrastructure was a basic ante of doing business—like leasing office space or putting in a telephone system. Yet computer technology had a background role. It was confined largely to desktop computers for employees and transaction systems that kept track of accounts, orders, and payments. Now, the Internet is changing the very nature of technology usage in large companies—and because of this, it is time for traditional companies to reassess how they manage technology.

THE NEW TECHNOLOGY DEPENDENCE

Dependence on computers is hardly new for consumer businesses. Since the 1960s, banks have relied entirely upon their mainframe computers to keep track of accounts, customer records, and balances. Banks such as Citibank that installed ATM machines early and took ownership positions in cash machine networks gained enormous competitive advantage. In retail, Wal-Mart famously used computers to upset the power balance between itself and Main Street stores by managing inventory better and turning it over faster—resulting in lower prices for consumers and greater market share for the company. In shipping, FedEx invented a whole new category with the development of overnight delivery—which was made possible only by computer logistics systems. In airline reservations, American gained market share by deploying the Sabre system to travel agents, initially making it easier to book American flights.

The Internet is forcing consumer companies to increase their dependence on computer technology by an order of magnitude. I'm acutely aware of this acceleration because as a technology industry analyst in the mid-1980s, I was, along with everyone else in my profession, on a mission to find the Holy Grail: a CIO who had used technology to achieve a real competitive advantage. Beyond a few notable exceptions in companies like Citibank, Wal-Mart, FedEx, and American Airlines, they were hard to find.

That's because most CIOs were *internally* focused. Their job was to keep "mission-critical" systems up and running: The telephones had to ring, the bank accounts needed be accessible at all times, networks had to have alternative routes, and transaction systems needed to recover from failure automatically. While this constituted a significant dependence on technology, it did not, in any real sense, change the strategy of most major companies.

There is, however, an enormous difference between mission-critical systems and *mission-redefining* technologies, which is how I would describe the role of *external,* or customer-facing, technologies such as Web sites. Granted, Web sites, like all mission-critical systems, must stay up and running. But more important, they embody the value, service, and brand of a company to customers. Because computer technology touches customers right at the point of sale and service, competitive strategy depends on computer technology as it never has before. Three factors make technology management today more challenging:

1: **Exogenous technology change**. Internet technology comes from outside of businesses themselves; it comes from the computer industry. As a result, consumer product-line managers, and particularly executives, lack expertise in the technologies they must continually master. In fact, many couldn't even be called well-versed laymen.

2: **Universal applicability.** Computer and networking technology is accelerating change around customer communication, points of sale, service, and product delivery—not product features. As a result, computer technology now affects a range of different industries all at once.

3: **Speed**. Computer technology advances at a stunning rate, and it is not likely to slow anytime soon. Each generation of processor chips grows exponentially faster and becomes cheaper to produce. That allows for further advances in hardware design, software, and networking technologies, which then consume that additional processing power. While almost every industry experiences periods of rapid technology change, the computer industry is fundamentally characterized by competition around technical innovation.

Business managers have always had to cope with technology change. Take the automobile industry, for example. Examine just one aspect of automobile design, such as safety, and you'll find a stream of continual innovation. First, seat belts were required, then shatterproof glass. Before long, consumers expected crumple zones at the front and rear to protect passengers. Next, it was antilock brakes, and then air bags to shield drivers and passengers in a collision.

Yet through all this technology change, the fundamental competitive structures of the automobile industry have remained more or less the same. General Motors, Ford, Toyota, and Volvo still operate with the same revenue mix and cost patterns they always have. Moreover, the technology changes that the automakers have had to assimilate in order to meet consumers' and regulators' expectations around safety have emanated largely from *inside* the industry, either from the car companies themselves or from their closely knit suppliers.

The *exogenous* change caused by the Internet will challenge automakers more than these industry-specific technology changes because, as we saw in Part Two, Internet technologies make it possible to change the *business model.* If a car maker achieves an advance in wheel traction, it may capture more market share in sport utility vehicles. A disruptive change, such as a significant move to electric cars, could topple industry leaders and bring new car makers to the fore. But these changes are product-specific and are, therefore, in a sense more contained than the ones introduced by the Internet.

On the Internet, competitors like AutoWeb and Auto-by-Tel attack the point of sale that connects consumers with dealers. They aggregate information about total demand, and they locate the cars that consumers want. In addition, automobile companies themselves are beginning to sell in a new way—direct. Once car companies can tell which models are wanted in advance, and where, the industry probably won't need all its dealers. Maybe the future auto industry will require huge regional car pickup centers, where consumers take possession of cars they have preordered on the Internet. Indeed, that is the scenario distribution entrepreneur Wayne Huizenga, founder of Blockbuster Video, is betting on with his new company, AutoNation.

The Internet is changing the roles of automobile makers, dealer networks, car magazines, referral sources, and car buyers in ways that cannot be completely foreseen. Companies that figure out how to use computer technology well have an unprecedented opportunity to gain market power.

Using computer technology to create a competitive advantage is a familiar idea, but actually doing it requires a relatively rare and critically important management skill. At Forrester, we call this management skill the *Whole View*, because it puts technology in the context of business rather than seeing it as a merely back-office utility.

THE WHOLE VIEW OF TECHNOLOGY MANAGEMENT

In the past, technology management has been essentially separate from the conduct of *real* business. This separateness was reflected in myriad ways. Most notably, CIOs and other technology managers have never been accorded the seniority, compensation, or status that customer-facing executives in sales, marketing, or product management have enjoyed. It's a rare traditional company whose most senior technology officer sits on its executive team. Frequently, the entire function of technology management is subordinated to the finance area.

This organization was in most cases entirely appropriate in an era when technology managers' main role was to keep transaction systems and employee PCs running. Yet it is mismatched to the realities of customer interaction in the Internet Economy. As more and more consumers do business on-line, the technology function not only touches the profit and loss statements of Internet companies but in fact embodies the entire consumer experience. Therefore, technology must be managed in tandem with both business strategy and consumer marketing.

In the Whole View, companies work to reduce and even eliminate the separations between marketing, business strategy, and technology—to manage all three as a continuous value-creation engine (see Figure 1). Four factors make Whole View technology management distinct from classical IT management:

1: **Direct consumer impact on company technology choices.** To offer an effective Web service, companies must mold their sys-

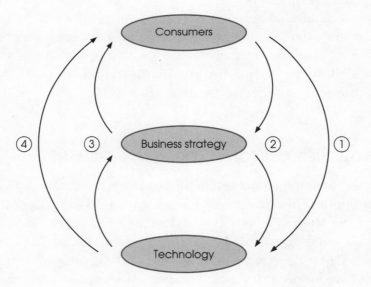

1. Direct consumer impact on company technology choices
2. Competitive market pressure to upgrade technology
3. Clear links between strategic options and technology know-how
4. Direct impact of technology skill upon consumer brand identity

Source: Forrester Research, Inc.

Figure 1 The Whole View of Technology Management

tems to the realities of consumer technology. Consumers arrive at a company's Web site with a set of personal technology, which a company must be able to connect to and serve. Companies must take into account what types of PC, palm computers, and telephones are installed in consumer homes. They must consider the speed of dial-up networking connections and understand the personal software setup of the consumers visiting their Web sites.

2: **Competitive market pressure to upgrade technology.** As we saw in chapter 6, Internet technology is creating an environment of Dynamic Trade, in which companies must match supply with current demand. To win, companies will have to build systems that can track and respond to consumer activity. Consumers' new demands upon companies generate new technology requirements.

3: **Clear links between strategic options and technology know-how.** In the past, many companies have essentially created business strategy in a technology vacuum. The basic assumption of non–technology executives was that technology was a lower-level "how to do it" issue, when they were playing a larger game of deciding "what to do." Yet technology enables so many new services and yet imposes such significant limitations that to have no grasp of the "how-to" literally makes it impossible to think clearly about what a company should do. What a company *can* offer its consumers, particularly in the area of service, depends mainly on computer technology.

4: **Direct impact of technology skill upon consumer brand identity.** As we saw in chapter 8, the Internet makes it possible to establish brands based more on *two-way experiences* than on *one-way projected images.* As experiential branding takes hold, the skill with which companies deploy computer technology will have a direct impact on consumer perception of their brand.

To adopt a Whole View with respect to technology management, companies must first reconsider the role of their technology leader. In some cases, classical IT leaders may not possess the characteristics required for Whole View technology management. Classical IT required dependable and efficient leaders. The best CIOs regularly cut costs and were able to get out new employee productivity systems or back-office applications on schedule. The effectiveness of a classical IT leader was measured by the percent of revenue spent on technology and the length of the "backlog," or applications waiting in a queue to be developed by the internal software team. Before the Internet, a CIO who could limit IT spending to just a few percent of revenues and manage the backlog to under eighteen months was a hero (see Figure 2).

Now, the technology management game has changed. While dependability and efficiency are still important, limiting technology

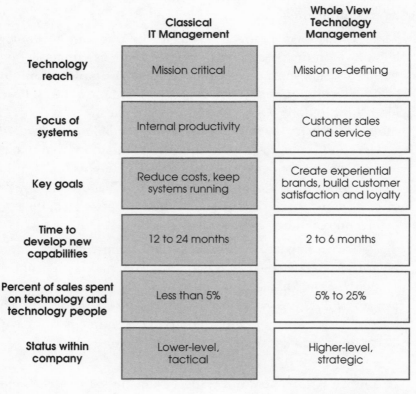

	Classical IT Management	Whole View Technology Management
Technology reach	Mission critical	Mission re-defining
Focus of systems	Internal productivity	Customer sales and service
Key goals	Reduce costs, keep systems running	Create experiential brands, build customer satisfaction and loyalty
Time to develop new capabilities	12 to 24 months	2 to 6 months
Percent of sales spent on technology and technology people	Less than 5%	5% to 25%
Status within company	Lower-level, tactical	Higher-level, strategic

Source: Forrester Research, Inc.

Figure 2 Classical IT versus Whole View Technology Management

expenses too much handicaps business strategy. A low-budget approach to the Internet can erode an established consumer brand. And running a backlog in development is out of the question in this fast-moving marketplace.

In addition, the Whole View requires a new set of skills from technology managers. To create a Whole View a company's technology leader must be a peer to his or her business strategy and marketing counterparts. Good technology leaders in the Internet Economy are not just dependable and efficient; they are also proactive in their approach to technology and influential within the executive team. As a proactive leader, this person must identify early which new technologies the company could wield in order to change its business model or respond to consumers.

At Forrester, we call this person the *New Technology Executive* because we believe that this breed is distinct from the classical CIO. A New Technology Executive possesses not only the background and skill to understand technology deeply; he or she also develops a broad and strategic understanding of the business as well. This individual is more likely to have risen through the organization on the business side and to have an MBA than to have started out as a software programmer. Yet neither is the New Technology Executive a technology neophyte.

Putting technology management in the hands of a marketing executive with no technology experience is just as bad a mistake as leaving it with a programmer-at-heart—maybe worse. Marketing executives who lack direct experience in technology can be taken in by the typical Silicon Valley sales pitch, which is usually long on vision but sometimes short on delivery. This can lead to a company making significant investments in technologies that simply aren't ready for the consumer market. Both technology and business skill sets are required of an executive who will be responsible for guiding technology's impact on strategy and, more important, for delivering the consumer's on-line experience.

Adopting a Whole View of technology management and choosing the right person to lead technology initiatives ensures that technology change is included in strategy making and that consumers' on-line experiences are delivered by people qualified to handle such a significant responsibility. Yet there remain two other important steps for a company that wants to thrive on technology change. The first is to clarify the company's relationship to technology—in other words, to decide when to build and when to buy technology. The second is to learn to identify when a consumer technology is ripe for the market.

CHOOSING A ROLE: VENDOR OR USER OF TECHNOLOGY

On the surface, it appears easy to tell which companies develop computer technology and which ones just buy and use it. But upon closer examination, a surprisingly high number of companies aren't clear about their relationship with technology. I recall a meeting that one of my Forrester colleagues and I had with a major media company to discuss its Internet investment strategy. The company asked us to provide a list of technology vendors that it should invest in directly.

For us, the answer was easy, and the list, short: none. Why? Because it was clear that the company had no core skill set in technology. Unless it planned a significant strategic shift, it would be better off as a *user* of technology, not a *vendor*. But we also knew that opening the meeting with such a conclusive statement would make it more difficult to persuade our clients to this view. So we prepared a list of some of the most interesting not-yet-public technology suppliers and braced ourselves for a difficult discussion. The vice president of business development began by telling the dozen or so people assembled that the company had passed on a chance to invest in Netscape. Had it invested, it would have earned over $50 million. He saw this meeting as an opportunity to identify the up-and-comers so that the company wouldn't make such a terrible mistake again.

With this as the backdrop, we set about our discussion. The problem was that half the people in the room had never heard of the companies we were discussing, and most had only the vaguest grasp of the technologies in question. Yet the story of Netscape—the "one that got away"—so overwhelmed them with regret that they pressed on, trying to sort good investment opportunities from bad ones.

The company's real problem was that it had never clarified its relationship to technology. Was it a *developer* of technology—a company with deep expertise in technology trends, with the kind of insight required of a venture capitalist? Or was it a technology *user*—a company that bought and deployed computers to create an effective Web business?

Like many others, this company couldn't decide on its role, so it ended up doing neither very well. Its Web site suffered from many flaws that slowed performance. And the company was also underqualified—and certainly not authorized—to be investing its shareholder's money in the computer industry. Such a move represented a radical diversification from its media roots. In the end, this company wisely pulled back from its technology investment program.

Saying that the company should have invested in Netscape is the equivalent of saying that it should have won the lottery. The odds of success for a non-technology company investing in technology are probably slightly better than that—but not by much. Companies that have profited most from Internet-oriented investments, such as CMG, Interpublic Group, Reuters, and Tribune Company, have focused their efforts around their own industries, where they have the contacts and the clout to help fledgling companies in which they have a stake.

The other source of confusion over a company's relationship to technology surrounds its Web site's software. When a company first launches a Web site, it will naturally license software from companies like Sun, Microsoft, Netscape, IBM, or Oracle to form the basis of the server system. But a lot of customization is required to define and program the site's features and its layout. As this work progresses, the line between developing technology and deploying it can become blurred.

Companies that begin by creating custom elements for their site sometimes go too far. I once visited a local television station where they told me, excitedly, that they had developed their own Internet search engine. The problem is, they really didn't need to build that technology. A whole range of suppliers offers search software—both for Internet and site-specific searches. Even companies with far bigger aspirations in search than the TV station, players such as Microsoft and Yahoo!, do not develop their own search engines.

Misplaced enthusiasm for "doing it yourself" can become very expensive. Quite a few consumer companies, particularly newspapers, found themselves in the Internet access business after they decided to help their consumers get on the Internet. What began as a small and exciting project quickly turned into a nightmare, as newspapers such as the *News & Observer* in Raleigh, North Carolina, found themselves operating banks of modems and fielding consumers' questions about dial-up networking. Worse, companies that entered the networking business soon discovered that the main competition was AT&T, UUnet, and MCI. When a price war began, the non-telecom players in Internet access suffered. Their losses grew with every customer they added.

What makes the build-or-buy divide so hard to manage is that companies that do, in fact, use technology to gain competitive advantage sometimes invest enormous amounts in technology. Many top Internet companies develop Web site capabilities that are superior to packaged-software offerings. If you look under the hood at Amazon, e.Schwab, or eBay, you'll find a commercial software base with a huge amount of internally developed code riding on top of it. Yet these leading users of technology will always prefer a less expensive, off-the-shelf package if it can meet their needs. They consistently look for ways to reduce internal development—even though they do more of it than most other companies.

At the end of the day, in order to manage technology well, consumer companies must first clarify their relationship to technology. Most consumer companies should be users, not vendors, of technology (see Figure 3). That means they should:

- Avoid blind investments in technology companies.
- Avoid building telecommunications infrastructure.
- Buy commercial software whenever possible, focusing all internal development on software that will differentiate the company and its Web site.

Vendor burden	User advantage
A vendor...	While a user...
must try to out-innovate all other technology players	buys best of breed
struggles to reduce costs of development	pays lowest market price
seeks to gain broad acceptance of proprietary technologies	benefits from industry-wide standardization

Source: Forrester Research, Inc.

Figure 3 Why Consumer Companies Should Avoid Becoming Vendors

DECIDING WHEN TECHNOLOGIES ARE RIPE FOR CONSUMER MARKETS

It is never easy, especially for consumer companies, to know with certainty which technologies will be hits and which will be costly mistakes. But there are some analytic tools that, if applied consistently, definitely increase the odds of choosing well.

In my experience, one of the most common mistakes that companies make is investing too much in immature technologies. For a company that is trying to think in radically new ways about its business, making premature bets is a significant risk. It may end up costing tens of millions of dollars.

Take Time Warner's investment in interactive television in 1995. At the time, the press was giving a lot of attention to "convergence"—the idea that television, personal computers, and telephones would all come together into a seamless network of communication. Convergence so seized the imaginations of the day that some huge mergers were predicated upon it. Viacom, for example, paid a premium for Paramount based on the notion that the archive of movies—the "content"—owned by Paramount would turn out to be a gold mine in the era of convergence. Consumers would pay to watch movies on demand. If that happened, another Viacom unit, Blockbuster Video, would be hit hard. In a world of convergence, it seemed to make sense to own the movies themselves.

One thing was clear: If consumers were going to watch movies on demand and perhaps even shop from their television sets, the network that connected TVs to the outside world would have to change radically. Instead of being connected to a one-way broadcast cable network, which carries TV signals to homes, interactive television would require a two-way switched network that could carry information back and forth.

To deliver those services, cable companies would have had to invest in a three-step upgrade of the cable infrastructure. First, they would have to upgrade the physical connections from pure coaxial cable to a combination of fiber and cable called "hybrid fiber-coax."[1] Second, to deliver movies on demand, cable operators would require switches that were capable of delivering a steady stream of audio and video. Yet the network would have to simultaneously carry intermittent signals such as electronic mail. Only the latest switch technology, called asynchronous transfer mode (ATM), could accomplish that.[2] Finally, consumers would require a new set-top box for their TVs. The one in place was designed to receive television signals. The new set-top box would have to be capable of two-way communication and of storing data and printing receipts.

Time Warner had good reason to think that interactive TV was a shrewd investment. As the largest owner of cable systems, it stood to benefit enormously from the ability to offer new services like movies on demand and shopping. Moreover, Time Warner's cable systems were clustered in major metropolitan areas, which gave it an advantage over a company like TCI, whose cable system operations covered the wide-open western states. Upgrading clustered cable systems would be less expensive, on a per-home basis, than reaching more remote areas.

Unfortunately, it was far too early to implement interactive TV.

To begin with, the technology was prohibitively expensive. By Forrester's estimate in 1995, it would have cost just over $1,200 per home to complete all three of the upgrades required. If Time Warner intended to recoup its cost by raising basic cable rates to $40 a month from $30, it would take ten years to break even. And at this time, regulators were reviewing and sometimes reducing cable rates.

Not only was interactive TV costly, but it barely worked. I attended the hoopla event that accompanied Time Warner's launch of the Full Service Network in Orlando. Visitors saw a presentation and demonstration by CEO Gerald Levin and were shown the "home of the future," which displayed the new services made possible by interactive television. Later, in the cafeteria, I overheard a group of engineers on loan for the event from Silicon Graphics, the high-end computer graphics workstation company that had, together with AT&T, provided much of the technology behind the Full Service Network. They were talking about the demo we'd seen that morning.

"I can't believe we pulled it off," said one. "Yeah, I was sure that as soon as Levin pushed the movie button, the whole thing would blow," said another. "I'm wiped out," said a third. Evidently, the team had been working around the clock for a week to get the demonstration to work. Convergence, it appeared, was not exactly ready for the consumer market.

Time Warner was not the only company to invest heavily in interactive television—nor will it be the last. At some point, when the technology works well and can be delivered cheaply enough, the idea, which has been kicking around for years, could suddenly become viable. Time Warner's mistake was not its *judgment* about interactive TV as an opportunity but the *timing* of its Full Service Network.

The main skill in deciding which new technologies matter and which ones don't, then, is correctly assessing their readiness for the market and the market's readiness for them. In practice, companies can increase their odds of making good technology decisions if they doggedly follow the three golden rules of technology timing (see Figure 4). Before betting on any technology, be sure that:

Question	Comments	Yes	No
Does it work?	New technologies must be easy enough for anyone to use without instruction. Networked products must work *at scale*, meaning with millions of concurrent users.	✔	☐
Is the cost reasonable?	Watch out for "magic numbers": • Avoid hardware products priced between $450 and $700 • Avoid basic network services that cost over $40 per month	✔	☐
Does it add clear value?	Value must be assessed relative to ease of use and cost. Technology optimists will see value where pessimists see none.	✔	☐

Source: Forrester Research, Inc.

Figure 4 Assessing the Market Readiness of New Consumer Technologies

- it works;
- its cost is reasonable; and
- it provides a clear value.

These rules may seem absurdly simple. But look at any major technology fiasco, and one or more of these rules has been violated.

In consumer markets, ease of use is probably the number one factor that determines timing. Not only must a technology work as promised, it must be easy enough for almost anyone to use. In the technology industry, many executives like to use the "Mom" test. "Could my mom use it?" they ask. The point is that *anyone* must be able to use the technology without instruction. Anything short of complete usability will land a technology in the hands of only a few dedicated *Fast Forwards* and exploratory *Mouse Potatoes*, missing mainstream consumers entirely.

Consider the Apple Newton, an early personal digital assistant, which hit the market in 1993. The theory of the Newton was revolutionary: Instead of being tied to their desks using PCs, businesspeople would track their contacts and appointments and take notes by carrying their computers with them. Yet in practice, using the Newton was awkward. The handwriting recognition feature didn't work very well, and the addresses and appointments that people recorded could not easily be transferred to and from PCs. 3Com's Palm Pilot, two product generations later, has been successful in large part because of its ease of use. The handwriting system works well enough to jot down notes, and Palm Pilot exchanges information with a PC with a single push of a button.

Another example of ease of use determining market timing comes from the on-line market. As far back as 1990, Prodigy offered an on-line service with a quasi-graphical interface. Although Prodigy used pictures, there was no consistent visual metaphor, as there is on a Macintosh or a Windows desktop. So even though Prodigy's presentation was far ahead of the blinking green characters of pre-Windows PCs, it wasn't good enough to attract any but the most enthusiastic computer users.

The breakthrough in on-line services came in 1993, when America Online introduced a Windows user interface. Suddenly on-line services were visually pleasing and easy to use. Interestingly enough, it took a competitor like CompuServe less than a year to catch up to America Online and introduce its own Windows versions. But the momentum that America Online generated through its ease of use propelled the company so far forward that others never caught up. Prodigy shrunk and refocused; CompuServe was bought by America Online in 1998; and other on-line services such as Delphi, Interchange, and GEnie and were bought out or faded into oblivion.

Beyond ease of use lies the issue of cost. Deciding what constitutes a reasonable cost for new technology can be very difficult—especially in consumer markets. While there is no hard evidence to support it, there seem to be some "magic numbers" in consumer technology—as there are in most consumer markets. There is no rational reason why a price of $3.99 sells so many more spiral notebooks than a price of $4.00. But it does. Consumers are attracted to—and repelled by—certain number patterns.

While these number patterns are not the only factor to consider when assessing the cost viability of consumer technology, they shouldn't be overlooked. In hardware products, for example, there appears to be a no-man's-land between $400 and $750 for any kind of computer or consumer electronics. Above this level, many consumers will invest in a technology with multiple uses, such as a PC. Below this range, consumers buy many single-purpose technology items such as game machines, cell phones, and palm computers. But in the middle, at $550 or $600, very few products sell well.

This is not to suggest that a consumer technology product *cannot* sell between $400 and $750, just that any proposed product at that level should raise a red flag. A hardware product priced in the middle range frequently turns out to be an immature technology that requires another generation—or two—of better and less expensive chip designs to become viable.

For consumer network services, the magic number seems to be $40 a month for any basic service. Internet access, cable, and new telephone services appear to be viable at $20 or $30 a month. But companies that have increased consumers' minimum monthly bills to over $40 a month for communication services seem to run into a wall. This is not to say that total bills cannot be larger. After all, long-distance voice charges frequently exceed this amount. Yet consumers seem to resist any basic connection that costs more than $40 a month.

Take as an example the difference between two high-speed Internet access services currently in the market—cable modem and ADSL, or high-speed dial. Cable modem Internet access costs just $39 a month in most cities, and it replaces a second phone line that would cost around $20 a month. High-speed dial is less widely available, and it costs $40 a month for the high-speed dial connection, plus another $15–20 for Internet service. Most consumers can't, or won't, pay the total of $55 for basic service—and thus ten times as many consumers use cable modems as use ADSL.

Of the three rules, deciding a technology's value is the most difficult. It's a "know it when you see it" thing. Optimists will see value in a technology that pessimists find to be completely unnecessary. Technologies that can establish absolute value—value measured in savings or convenience—have the best shot at success. If cable modem service can connect a consumer to the Internet a hundred times faster than regular dial-up, yet costs just $10 more per month (still falling under the magic number of $40), that's clear value. Likewise, an MP3 player that allows a teenager access to cheap or free music offers clear value.

The other factor that makes value tough to judge is that it can be established only relative to ease of use and price. The more a technology requires consumers to change their behavior, the harder it is to use, and the more expensive, the more clearly compelling the value must be.

One technology that has repeatedly failed the value test despite a seemingly huge appeal is video phone calls. Some might argue that there is a considerable value in being able to see the person with whom you're speaking. But the amount of value *over and above hearing their voice* has never been compelling enough to get companies or consumers past the hassle of using cameras in their daily communications. Companies using videoconferencing have to set aside space for the videoconference equipment. Consumers have to mount a camera on their PCs, where it seems to stare at you like some strange Cyclops. Moreover, most companies and consumers have not been willing to pay effectively double the telecommunications cost of their voice calls in order to get video.

RETHINKING THE ROLE OF TECHNOLOGY AND TECHNOLOGY MANAGERS

The rise of new media and electronic commerce has caused a technology divide in many large organizations. Frequently, the IT department, keeper of the mission-critical systems, was not the group that began experimenting with the Internet as a customer-facing technology. More often, that role has fallen to the marketing department.

In part, this happened because early Web sites were little more than electronic brochures. Frankly, IT managers considered the Web to be a trivial technology—one without any real impact on the core business systems. Marketers assumed responsibility for manag-

167

ing the Web site, and in many cases marketing is where the Internet initiative still resides.

That arrangement has caused several problems that are just now gaining the attention of managers in large companies. First, the marketing department usually isn't very technology-savvy. And thus we frequently find consumer companies that invest rashly in technology companies or begin reinventing technology that could be purchased for less money. Moreover, marketing groups often poorly assess the reliability and maturity of the software they *do* purchase.

Second, the IT departments of many large companies have been bypassed in electronic commerce. This phenomenon has created, in some cases, an underclass of technology employees who run older systems but are not encouraged to participate in the development of the company's Internet business. Meanwhile, the market for Internet technical talent is in a frenzy. Software developers now expect—and regularly command—high salaries, stock options, flexible hours, and extra vacation from companies desperate for their expertise. In short, traditional companies must turn their attention to improving the way they manage their technology skills and people.

In this shift, Forrester advocates a Whole View of technology management over a classical IT approach. In the Whole View, technology is tied more closely with business strategy and consumer branding. To create an effective Whole View, companies must be clear about whether they are vendors or users of technology. In most cases, consumer companies should avoid trying to become developers of technology. Instead, they should rely on the stream of innovation that naturally emanates from competition in the computer industry. Finally, consumer companies need to develop skills in identifying which technologies are ready for consumer markets and which ones need years, or even decades, before they'll appeal to the average consumer.

In the next chapter, we'll explore the second major challenge that traditional companies face because of the Internet: channel conflict. For any company that sells through distributors and retailers, the Internet is creating tremendous pressure to go direct. In chapter 10, we'll look at how some companies have solved this sticky issue and see which channel strategies work best.

CHAPTER 10

Coping with Internet Channel Conflict

For traditional manufacturers, channel conflict is the thorniest issue of all on the Internet.[1] On the one hand, the Internet seems like good news—a way to reach more people and sell more products. On the other hand, the manufacturer's retailers and distributors will object in the strongest possible way to any efforts the company makes to sell direct on the Internet or to support new dotcom retailers.

Sometimes, the fear of channel retaliation can go so far as to warp the entire Internet strategy of a manufacturer. I know a West Coast clothing maker, for example, whose retail partners objected so vociferously to the company's strategy of selling on-line that it pulled its products from its Internet site. Instead of selling on its site, as the company had originally planned, it posts descriptions of its latest designs and a guide to stores in various areas. This guide does not show what products are actually available, either—just the names of retailers that carry any part of the company's product line.

This action is surprising because the apparel maker had never before caved in to its retailers' demands. In fact, this company had traditionally sold through its own stores as well as through franchisees and other retailers. The apparel brand itself was strong enough that the manufacturer never needed to grant geographic exclusivity for its products to its third-party partners. Yet here it was, cowed by Internet channel conflict.

After the traditional retailers forced the company to stop selling on its own Web site, they went a step further, demanding that it decline to sell on any Internet start-up site. They argued that the Internet should be considered an extension of their existing relationship with the manufacturer, and so they should be the only ones authorized to sell its clothing on the Internet. Once again, the company conceded to its retailers.

I met the VP of electronic commerce for this company at about the time its entire Internet strategy of selling exclusively through existing retailers was falling apart. As it turned out, none of the company's traditional retail partners or franchisees had managed to build an effective Web presence. The manufacturer was dismayed to find other makers racing ahead in Internet sales because they had more effective channel strategies.

Not only had appeasement failed to create Internet sales, but the company was finding it harder and harder to enforce its policy. "Our products show up all the time on sites we've never even heard of," the VP of e-commerce told me. "We don't even know how these new Internet sites are sourcing our products—it looks to us like they're going through our secondary distributors." The problem was that every time one of this company's major retailers spotted its products on a new Web site, it called to complain—sometimes directly to the office of the president. "It's outrageous," the VP of electronic commerce said. "We're letting our traditional retailers cut us off from the Internet, which is our best potential source of new growth."

The apparel maker's experience offers a good example of how aggressive and harmful traditional retail channel partners can be when it comes to the Internet. But when this clothing company bent to accommodate its retailers, it failed to consider how this strategy affected the on-line experience of its consumers. Not only have retailers hurt the company's growth prospects, but they are also delivering a frustrating experience to its consumers—damaging the clothing brand in the process.

For the consumer, trying to buy this brand of clothing on the Internet is disappointing at best. Technographics research shows that consumers begin their Internet shopping trips at search sites, where they seek out a particular brand or product. If the manufacturer had continued to sell on its own site, perfecting the search results for its brands would have been an immediate priority. But since the clothier's site is nothing more than a brochure, the company paid no attention to this process. As a result, the company's consumers must sift through ten or twenty vaguely related listings at the search site, looking for the real brand.

Once consumers get to the manufacturer's site, they expect to be able to buy the clothing. Instead, they get marketing . . . and marketing . . . and more marketing. Finally, consumers realize that in order to buy, they must visit one of the retailers listed on the site—so they click on those names. At this point, they discover that some of the stores listed on the site haven't set up a Web presence at all, while others have sites so slow and incomplete that there is no hope of finding, much less buying, the product. Disgusted, the Internet consumer finally leaves—perhaps never to return.

MANAGING TRUCULENT RETAILERS

The chief problem with selling solely through traditional bricks-and-mortar retailers that have moved to the Web is that, as a group, they're not very good at it. Forrester's research on retail sites finds that the Internet versions of bricks-and-mortar stores lag behind both catalog merchants and Internet start-ups in total site budget, speed, number of SKUs, site features, and customer service. In the apparel industry, for example, Forrester's study of forty on-line clothing sellers revealed that catalog merchants and Internet-only retailers offered a significantly more complete product set on-line than traditional bricks-and-mortar retailers (see Figure 1).

For a manufacturer that sells the majority of its products through bricks-and-mortar retailers, this relative weakness represents a significant disadvantage in reaching Internet consumers.

Yet it is rarely to the manufacturer's advantage to snub its bricks-and-mortar partners. After all, Internet sales still represent only a

171

Description	CATALOG Majority of revenue from catalog sales (may have stores)	PURE PLAY Sells on-line only	BRICK-AND- MORTAR RETAILER Majority of revenue from physical stores	MANUFACTURER Sells only in stores owned by others	MANUFACTURER HYBRID Sells both in own stores and others'
Number interviewed	6	12	12	3	7
Median number of SKUs available online	10,000	12,000	1,000	110	550
Offers online order tracking	60%	42%	42%	33%	29%
Accepts in-store returns	75%	N/A	92%	N/A	43%
Uses in-store kiosks	20%	N/A	50%	N/A	29%

Percent of 40 on-line apparel retailers responding

Source: Forrester Research, Inc.

Figure 1 Channel Structure of 40 Apparel Sellers

tiny fraction of the overall total in every consumer-goods category. Annoyed retailers won't hesitate to pull a manufacturer's products off the shelves in their stores if they perceive an effort to undermine their retail franchise. One client of mine quite aptly calls this "the Wal-Mart Factor." Major retailers like Wal-Mart account for such a high percentage of sales that no manufacturer is willing to enrage them.

Instead, manufacturers must use a combination of push and pull to get traditional retailers going on the Internet. The push comes in the form of an indirect, but clearly implied, threat to sell direct. To accomplish this push, the manufacturer must set up some form of direct sales over the Internet. Ideally, this direct-selling site will target *new customers,* ones the traditional retail partners do not currently serve, or it will sell *new value*—a product or service that the traditional partners have no right to expect to control (see Figure 2).

One site that explicitly targets new customers, for example, is Estée Lauder's Clinique site, which sells makeup and skin-care products. Launched in late 1998, the Clinique site expanded rapidly. By

172

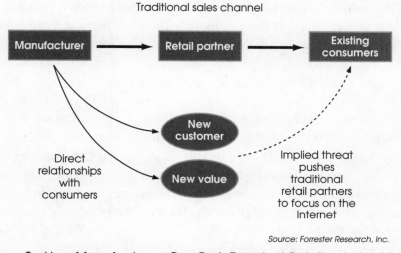

Source: Forrester Research, Inc.

Figure 2 How Manufacturers Can Push Truculent Retailers to be More Effective On-line

mid-1999, Clinique had registered more than two hundred thousand new customers—people who had never used the brand before or were lapsed customers. This represents 30 percent of the site's total registrants. By signing up on the Web site, these new consumers are saying, in effect, "I am interested in Clinique." As it turns out, the great majority of these new customers actually end up buying the product at retail.

Angela Kapp, vice president and general manager for Estée Lauder on-line, says, "Channel conflict is a highly charged emotional issue, but the fact is that over 90 percent of the people visiting Clinique on-line aren't transacting there. In some cases, we haven't convinced them to buy, but most are gathering information before going to the store." In fact, in one of Clinique's studies, 68 percent of the women registered at the Web site said that they'd rather purchase skin cream at the department store than on-line. Says Kapp, "The point is, if we can attract new consumers to the brand through the Web site, it helps our department stores just as much as it helps us."

From the retailer's point of view, the addition of so many potential new buyers of the brand can only be positive. After all, most of these on-line visitors end up buying the products at a retail outlet.

Yet the fact that Clinique sells direct on-line also sends a message to retailers. Even though the company's Internet revenues are infinitesimal in the context of Estée Lauder's $4 billion beauty business, the sheer fact that Clinique *can* sell direct lets retailers know that they have to get going on the Internet.

One good way to target new customers on the Internet is to aim for a different Technographics group from the one that traditional retail partners serve. For example, Martha Stewart, the doyenne of home décor, could target high-income optimists on-line while serving lower-income pessimists in the retail channel. This strategy is made easier by the fact that the company already segments consumers into different channels. The buyers of Martha Stewart–branded sheets and towels at Kmart are mainstream consumers. Yet Martha By Mail, the company's catalog, is decidedly up-market—featuring items such as gardening tools and fine linen guest towels. This company can effectively sell to the early adopter group on-line without disturbing its mass-market retail relationships much.

New value might take the form of a separate product line, designed solely for sales over the Internet. Or it might take the form of a service, such as regular replenishment for makeup or pantyhose, repairs and maintenance in the case of durable goods, or member benefit clubs for convenience goods like apparel.

By choosing a new customer and a new value, the manufacturer defines the *revenue mix* of its Internet business in such a way that it does not directly interfere with its current retailer relationships. Yet this strategy also sends a clear message to retailers that they must participate fully on the Internet if they want to remain partners.

The pull of getting retailers on-line involves assisting longtime partners to ensure that they—and by association the manufacturer—do not get left behind on the Internet. Manufacturers can construct a support program specifically aimed at getting key sellers on-line and up to speed as quickly as possible. At the same time, the manufacturer must make it clear that it will not allow its product to be sold through clumsy Web sites any more than it would consent to sell through badly managed retail stores. Executing this Internet strategy consists of four steps:

1: **Set a standard.** Manufacturers should declare that any Web site must meet certain minimum standards in order to sell their products on-line. These standards could include basic site performance, ability to deliver product as promised, consistency, accuracy, completeness of product presentation, or any other factor that the manufacturer feels is important to meeting the consumer's expectations around the brand, shopping experience, and pricing.

2: **Build relationships with Internet-only retailers.** Manufacturers can learn a lot by advertising and selling products through the most leading-edge Internet retail sites. Because start-ups badly need both the revenue and cachet that a major advertiser brings, the manufacturer will be in a position to visit and learn about the state of the art in Internet store operations. In so doing, the manufacturer can identify the most significant deficits in the activities of its traditional retailers on-line and can better define the minimum standards that it will require of its on-line partners.

3: **Help traditional partners**. Once they have learned from leading-edge Internet retailers what tactics work best selling their products on-line, manufacturers can help their traditional partners tremendously by offering feedback on what their sites do well and where they need to invest more. Manufacturers can offer cooperative marketing dollars to fund traditional partners' sites, and they can create promotions that span the physical store and on-line venues, thus helping traditional retailers capitalize on their key strengths.

4: **Disqualify traditional retailers that fail to keep up.** This is the hardest step in managing traditional retailers effectively on the Web. It is also the most critical. Many traditional retailers believe that because they have sold a certain manufacturer's

175

products in their stores, they have a special right to carry those same products on the Web. Many will be shocked if they are prevented from doing so. Yet as difficult as that situation is, the manufacturer can handle it with finesse by doing everything in its power to help slower traditional partners get back on track. This assistance could include anything from helping to arrange adequate Web site funding to reviewing and testing the site in cooperation with the retailer. But if that approach doesn't work, you must cut your on-line ties with them.

BUILDING RELATIONSHIPS WITH INTERNET-ONLY RETAILERS

In addition to encouraging existing retailer partners to create an effective Web strategy, consumer-goods manufacturers should explicitly seek out relationships with new dotcom retailers. In theory, this should be easy. After all, new Internet retailers are eager to sell products and benefit from cooperative marketing efforts with manufacturers. However, manufacturers have been reluctant to develop new Internet channel relationships—and not just because of possible reprisal from store chains.

Manufacturers fear becoming secondary casualties if bricks-and-mortar retailers lose the battle for Internet consumers. The relationships that manufacturers have with major store chains, often won through years of hard work and negotiation, represent an important competitive advantage vis-à-vis other product makers. If traditional retailers lose ground to Internet start-ups, then the manufacturers with the best in-store shelving arrangements, end-cap displays, and promotions stand to lose out, too. Indeed, that's why many manufacturers want the Internet to go away as much as traditional retailers do.

The problem is that selling only through traditional channel partners limits the manufacturer's Internet strategy too much. Consider, for example, some of the choices facing one pet supplies maker. This company has traditionally sold its products through grocery chains, pet shops, and superstores. Strong store relationships have been an important source of its strategic advantage. For this company, as for many consumer-goods makers, having ready access to limited shelf space has been a key success factor.

The company knew it had to build a Web site, but it wanted to do so in a way that was favorable to its traditional channel partners. Its solution was to build a site that offered friendly tips on pet training, ideas for activities, and information for enthusiasts of various breeds. The company decided firmly not to sell its products on-line in order to honor its existing retail relationships.

For a while, this Web strategy seemed to yield a win for both the manufacturer and its retail partners. The manufacturer's site attracted thousands of current customers. The information these consumers got on the site built greater brand allegiance, and that clearly supported the company's sales at retail. In addition, the pet supplies maker began to sell a few of its products through start-up Internet retailers and, in some cases, to advertise on those sites. But these were minor activities in the overall scope of the business.

Soon, however, the pet supplies space began to heat up on-line. Start-ups such as Pets.com, PetStore.com, PetsMart, and Petopia aimed directly at traditional pet stores. These sites not only offered tips and information but also sold pet food, leashes, cages, treats, and all the other items that pet owners need to buy. In addition, on-line grocers such as NetGrocer, Peapod, WebVan and Streamline added pet supplies to their list of products for sale. When Amazon bought Pets.com in the spring of 1999, it suddenly became clear that Internet retailers were not just a tangential aspect of the pet business; they were an important challenge to the structure of the industry.

The changing on-line landscape presents this manufacturer with some tough choices. On the one hand, the advent of a new channel is good news—offering the possibility of increased sales. On the other hand, the economics of Internet businesses suggest that, in the end, there will be just a few big sellers on-line. There is a substantial risk to the manufacturer that one of the start-ups will emerge as a dominant player, with just one or two principal Internet competitors in the pet supply business. In that case, these few players could control almost all of the manufacturer's sales over the Internet. They could, in essence, end up commanding the equivalent of shelf space in the on-line world—customer accounts.

The key question, then, is how much of the pet supply business is going to move on-line? Technographics offers quite a clear picture. Looking at buyers of pet food—who, it is safe to assume, are largely the same people who buy other pet supplies—reveals that, depending on the brand, 35 to 40 percent are *early adopters*.[2] This suggests that our manufacturer does need to be concerned about the possibility of a powerful set of dotcom retailers emerging.

This manufacturer is well positioned to expand its relationships with Internet pet stores because it has been in the market almost since the beginning. But how far should the company go in supporting these new players? The manufacturer must guard against letting dotcom retailers gain too much power. That means it must push traditional retailers to move on-line faster, and it must support as many Internet intermediaries as possible.

Building a range of Internet channel partnerships may be difficult for some traditional managers, who are accustomed to choosing a few most favored retailers within each geographic area. On the Internet, there is no geographic area. Instead, the goal of a manufacturer's Internet distribution strategy should be to *maximize* the number of different partners carrying its products to Internet consumers. These new Internet partners should include dotcoms that intend to scale up their business, as Amazon's Pets.com clearly does in the pet supply arena, as well as many smaller affiliate partners who may refer sales to the manufacturer or its distributors.

In the case of our pet products supplier, Internet affiliates might include veterinarians, dog trainers, pet store owners, breeders, and other individuals in small businesses who could supplement their incomes with pet supply sales. In the past, these individuals would have been less likely to sell products because of the difficulty and cost of stocking and delivering the goods. But, as we saw in earlier chapters, the Internet also makes it cheaper for very small businesses to operate.

SELLING DIRECT

In addition to encouraging traditional retail partners and cultivating new Internet retailers and sales affiliates, most manufacturers should probably sell direct over the Internet, even if they never have before. There are several reasons.

First, consumers expect it. In the past, the only time consumers ever saw a company like Mattel was on television, in print advertisements, and at retail. The company itself was an abstract entity, a business that consumers simply never touched. On the Internet, consumers have a very different experience. When they go to their favorite search sites, they enter brand names such as "Barbie dolls." Search results point them to Mattel's Barbie Web site, and consumers naturally assume that it is the best place to get a Barbie. How they are disappointed! When the consumer arrives at the site, the only Barbie dolls available are the collectors' versions, the ones that look like Audrey Hepburn in *Breakfast at Tiffany's*. Regular Barbie dolls aren't for sale—yet.

Second, Dynamic Trade offers greater benefits to direct sellers than to indirect sellers. Companies that touch consumers directly will have greater market power in the Internet Economy, where power derives principally from delivering positive brand experiences, controlling physical product delivery, and acting on information about current demand. Companies that sell exclusively through others miss the opportunity to develop their own sense about what Internet consumers want. Moreover, they risk empowering large dotcom retailers by allowing them to become the sole sources of aggregate consumer demand information.

Third, the cost reductions made possible by the Internet apply only to direct sellers. Direct sellers can promote cheaply through e-mail, slash the cost of taking orders, and extend their reach to new places without adding new physical locations. This helps any company, be it a retailer or a catalog merchant, that sells to consumers on the Internet. Manufacturers that sell only through others stand to gain nothing from the Internet on the cost side.

The idea of selling direct to consumers is so radical that some manufacturers dismiss it out of hand. However, my experiences working with consumer companies that sell direct over the Internet show that, in fact, they are usually taken aback by how many consumers go right ahead and buy from them. This experience reflects in part the Technographics of Internet consumers in 1999. More than 60 percent of Internet buyers are high income optimists—people willing to change their behavior and to buy items directly, even those they've never bought that way before.

The direct-selling experience of one manufacturer, a large and diversified company whose products span a wide range of branded household goods and personal-care products, stands out in my mind. Before the Internet, this company had sold mainly through retailers and distributors. But on-line, the company listed all its products and offered them for sale—just to see what would happen. When we met to discuss the company's Internet strategy, the CEO confessed that he was shocked by how much they were able to sell. The company had viewed its Web effort as purely experimental and thus had done little promotion. But remarkably enough, consumers searched for the company's products and found its site.

Even more intriguing was the mix of products consumers bought on-line. The company had expected to sell only the more expensive items whose shipping cost would be low compared with the product price. Yet it turned out that the Fast Forwards and Mouse Potatoes buying household products on-line in 1999 were utterly focused on convenience. These early adopters would literally pay a dollar of shipping on a $5 item to save time.

Realizing that he might be able to build a very large business selling direct on-line, the CEO had to decide how far and how fast he should grow that channel. How much should the company invest in an electronic commerce site that sells direct? So far, the company had been able to keep its technology expenditures low by letting a third party host the site. Product shipping had been a patchwork trial system—good enough to test consumer response, but in no way capable of scaling up to over a hundred million in sales, which is where this CEO thought he could go.

As we spoke, it became increasingly clear that to sell direct, this company would not be able to avoid investing substantially more—tens of millions of dollars more—in its Web site. Most likely, this company would also need to find a fulfillment partner that could pick, pack, and ship Internet orders.

Because of the difficulty and cost of expanding its Web site, the company seriously considered pulling back from direct sales and just referring consumers to other on-line stores. However, a review of the sites put up by the company's traditional partners revealed appalling slowness, poor presentation, and even outright inaccuracy in product descriptions and pricing. Internet start-ups also presented the company's products poorly. In fact, at one Internet start-up site, consumers were being offered a discount on a product that the manufacturer had recently recalled for safety reasons. Referring Internet consumers to these sites could prove to be a costly and brand-damaging mistake.

This story illustrates that sometimes a manufacturer discovers that it must sell direct on the Internet in order to satisfy the its customers' needs. This manufacturer had—and still has—no intention of abandoning its longtime retail partners. At the same time, it would benefit from developing new on-line retail relationships. And it would be better to have some control in the presentation of its products through dotcom retailers. But in the end, the only way for this company to understand how consumers behave on-line and what they will buy is to sell direct over the Internet.

CHANNEL STRATEGIES FOR DYNAMIC TRADE

From the manufacturer's point of view, then, an effective Internet channel strategy combines traditional retailers, new dotcom retailers, smaller Internet affiliates, and direct sales. The question is how to balance these different channels to ensure a good experience for consumers and the best possible sales distribution for the manufacturer. In other words, what mix of these channels should the manufacturer target?

There is no single correct answer to this question. Some manufacturers will lean toward the on-line stores of their traditional retailers; others will balance traditional retailers more evenly with Internet-only companies. Affiliates may be a good choice in industries like pet supplies, where a large number of individual professionals exist to form the affiliate layer, but affiliate programs may be inappropriate for other consumer goods. Many manufacturers will sell direct, but some will find reasons why they must not on any account sell their own products.

What is clear is that the manufacturer must build an overall Internet channel system that performs consistently across these choices. A manufacturer should not really care whether its product is sold through a traditional retailer, a dotcom retailer, an affiliate, or on its own Web site.

The best way for a manufacturer to balance the various Internet sales channels is to separate Internet channel partners based on the value that they add to the sales process (see Figure 3). The first step is to divide the value provided by Internet intermediaries into the three services they perform:

1: **Finding the consumer.** The first step in the sales process is to locate a consumer. Small Internet affiliates can perform this role, as can larger Internet-only retailers and the Internet stores of traditional partners. The value of generating a sales lead will vary by industry, but in most cases it will be limited to around 5 percent of the value of a sale.

2: **Transacting the sale and providing service.** Taking a customer order, processing the payment, letting the consumer know when delivery can be expected, and handling complaints from purchases gone awry all form the second element of value provided by intermediaries. This level of service is worth more than simply generating leads, since these functions form the bulk of the consumers' experience on-line. Intermediaries that perform transactions and provide service should earn more than pure lead generators do—perhaps more like 15 percent of a sale.

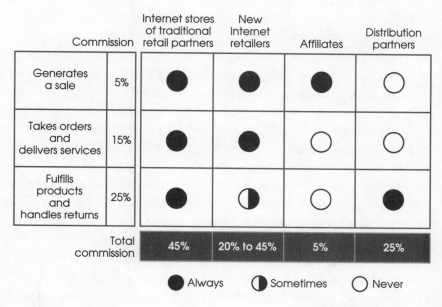

Commission		Internet stores of traditional retail partners	New Internet retailers	Affiliates	Distribution partners
Generates a sale	5%	●	●	●	○
Takes orders and delivers services	15%	●	●	○	○
Fulfills products and handles returns	25%	●	◑	○	●
Total commission		45%	20% to 45%	5%	25%

● Always　◑ Sometimes　○ Never

Source: Forrester Research, Inc.

Figure 3　Distribute Commission Base on Channel Partners' Services

3: **Holding inventory and delivering product.** Warehousing inventory, packing goods for shipment, and arranging timely delivery are expensive services for intermediaries to provide. Not only that, but product shipment and delivery done well build a positive brand experience, while bungling this aspect of the consumer's experience can drive the buyer back to bricks-and-mortar retail outlets faster than any other kind of mistake. Consequently, inventory and delivery functions should earn an even higher percent of sales—in many cases, as much as 25 percent.

A *physical* retail channel partner like Macy's department store provides all three services. The consumer shops with the assistance of store clerks and buys there. Macy's puts the product into the consumer's hands. Later, if the consumer doesn't like what she bought, she can return the product to Macy's. On the Internet, a manufacturer's channel partners can do any or all of these activities.

Imagine, for example, that generating a lead on a sale is worth 5 percent of the sale; actually taking the order and providing service is worth 15 percent; and stocking inventory and delivering products is worth 25 percent. If the manufacturer sells and fulfills that product itself, it pays nothing to channel partners. If the manufacturer sells the product on its Web site but relies on a third-party distribution partner to handle fulfillment, it would pay 25 percent for this behind-the-scenes service. If the manufacturer sells through the Internet site of a traditional retailer that finds the consumer, takes the order, manages product delivery, and handles product returns at the store, the manufacturer would pay the full 45 percent commission. To an Internet affiliate that merely refers the sale, the maker would pay just 5 percent.

An important part of the math in this type of Internet channel strategy is aligning the commissions paid to the costs incurred. Carrying inventory and handling physical products are the most expensive activities, so they win the highest commissions. Closing on-line sales and providing service is next, while generating leads is least expensive. By matching the commissions to the costs incurred at each level of the sales process, the manufacturer becomes financially indifferent among its partners. That means the manufacturer can stop worrying about which type of partner sells its product over the Internet and can concentrate on how it will respond to its total current demand.

Developing a consistent system of this nature also allows a manufacturer to support its traditional retailers on an absolute commission basis. Because traditional retailers will be at the top of the chain—selling, delivering product, and providing service—they qualify for the whole 45 percent commission in this model. Yet this channel strategy still leaves room for the manufacturer to cultivate dotcoms and affiliates as well.

Finally, this system balances the power of the dotcoms by allowing for the development of both traditional retail partners and affiliates on-line. Without these alternate sellers, manufacturers risk being subjugated by a few superscale Internet retailers. Balancing the power of Internet channel partners against one another and seeking the largest possible number of Internet points of sale is the manufacturer's best strategy.

This concludes our look at the issue of Internet channel conflict. In the next chapter of *Now or Never* we'll look at the gravity that surrounds traditional companies of all kinds with respect to funding and leadership. We'll look at why traditional companies' Internet businesses are chronically underfunded when compared with start-up Internet challengers. We'll consider why traditional companies have so much difficulty retaining qualified management talent to help them build their Internet businesses. And we'll examine the role of the CEO and why, in some cases, the leader slows the organization down so much that it cannot become competitive on the Internet. Finally, we'll look at how companies can solve these challenges through funding, organizational, and leadership change.

CHAPTER 11

Funding, Organization, and Leadership

In theory, the fact that Internet businesses generate losses for the first few years should confer an advantage on incumbents in consumer markets. After all, companies with an existing customer base, a well-known brand, actual revenues, and profits from the traditional business ought to be in a much better position to cross-subsidize an Internet effort. But in reality, it doesn't work that way.

Instead, large companies usually lag behind newly formed ventures that have nowhere near as many resources. It is as if traditional companies are caught in a gravitational field, which constantly pulls them backward toward the industry's age-old business practices. To win the battle for Internet consumers, traditional companies must break free of this gravity. They need to fight as if they have everything to lose.

WHY TRADITIONAL COMPANIES LAG BEHIND

A manager of a traditional business who has been given the mandate to "create an Internet unit" finds the hypergrowth of electronic commerce daunting. Sales over the Internet in many cases grow at rates much higher than anyone predicts. Simultaneously, Internet start-ups challenge the traditional revenue mix and prices begin to fall. Managing all these dynamics at once can prove overwhelming for someone who has built a career over more than a decade of relative stability in his or her industry.

I first recognized this problem when one of Forrester's clients, a retailer, asked us to review his Internet business plan. The company had been selling on-line for more than a year, but it was preparing to gear up its efforts to go after the Internet opportunity aggressively. Our client wanted to be sure he had the plan in order because he was going to ask his company's board to approve a request for funding.

When I began to review the plan before our scheduled meeting, it was immediately obvious that our whole discussion would have to revolve around growth. The plan forecasted a growth projection of 75 percent, compounded over the first three years—in a market growing much faster than that.

The meeting with our client was difficult from the start. We began by pointing out that the prevailing revenue growth rate in the retailer's sector in 1997–1998 was over 500 percent—yes, that's a five-fold increase. The best of the traditional players were posting increases of 250 percent or more that year, and some Internet start-ups were growing three times that rate. This retailer's forecast for a 75 percent increase meant that it was actually planning to lose market share on the Internet. And we were not talking about inconsequential numbers here, either—the categories this retailer addressed together sold over $1 billion electronically in 1998.

After hearing our analysis of his market, our client sat back and said, "You've got to understand, these guys [the board] are looking at a retail business that's been growing at a few percentage points per year—in the good years. There's no way they're going to approve an Internet plan that calls for over a hundred percent revenue growth. And if they did, they'd hold me to it. How can I be sure it'll happen? I've built a career on doing what I said I was going to do. I'm not going to stop now. If I plan 75 percent and deliver 100, I'll be a hero. But if I plan for 250 percent and fall short, they'll replace me."

Unfortunately, this manager's assessment is all too true. For traditional company managers, it is far less risky to underperform on the Internet than to try to excel. Not spoken, but looming as a truth in the room, was the fact that he had no personal incentive to push his business to the limit. Granted, he owned company stock, but its value was tied to the traditional business, not this Internet unit.

This manager's situation underscores what is, in fact, an epidemic at large traditional companies: lack of leadership for the Internet. More often than not, what you find at major corporations is a small group, which sometimes includes gifted people, trying to devise an Internet strategy for the company. But rarely does this group have enough authority from the CEO or the board to reconstruct the business as required for the Internet.

What is happening in these cases is nothing short of a complete breakdown of leadership. The company's CEO, president, and board have failed to tell employees what the company's Internet objective is. No doubt, many of these leaders are uncertain what the strategy should be, and they feel they do not have the time to figure it out. So they create a team of employees responsible for answering the question, What should we do on the Internet?

Next, one of two scenarios unfolds. The first is that the employee team is led by an able manager, who concludes that the company needs to take very bold steps—putting existing distribution arrangements at risk, perhaps rethinking the business model, and so on. But when the uninvolved CEO or president hears the team's analysis, the recommendations seem so outlandish that no authority or funding to pursue the effort is granted. At that point, our very able manager, having persuaded himself that the Internet will transform his industry, often chooses to leave—usually to join a dotcom competitor.

The second, more typical, scenario is that a weak manager leads the Internet strategy team. This individual either fails to grasp the business implications of the Internet or lacks the guts to communicate them to a skeptical CEO. This situation arises in part because traditional companies—with no initial public offering ahead—are unable to lure the kind of ambitious and driven executives one finds at the helm of the dotcom contingent. And traditional companies often fail to put the best of their internal people on the Internet task. After all, goes the thinking, why put your star player on your farm team? Smart up-and-coming executives avoid the Internet, recognizing that if their CEO is ambivalent, then leading electronic commerce is a potential career wrecker. In both scenarios, the result of no leadership is the same: paralysis, and no clear action plan for the Internet.

CREATING A SEPARATE ORGANIZATION DOES NOT ALWAYS SOLVE THE PROBLEM

Faced with the challenges of hypergrowth, new business models, and downward price pressure, many large companies form a separate unit for their Internet activities. A separate unit, they reason, will be able to respond more quickly to the turbulent market. And it also allows the company to grant managers stock options as incentives. Creating a separate unit often solves these issues, but not always.

Even separate units can be too closely tied to the traditional company's ways of doing business. Consider the case of CareerPath.com, a company established in 1995 by a group of newspapers including the *LA Times, Boston Globe, San Jose Mercury News, New York Times, Washington Post,* and *Chicago Tribune.*[1] The idea behind CareerPath was a great one—the site would roll together all the job listings of more than twenty newspapers nationwide to create a national uber-database of available positions. No start-up could match the number of jobs that these local papers could aggregate. Yet despite this clear advantage, CareerPath ran into trouble early on. Even though it was technically a separate entity, CareerPath reported to a board of newspaper owners. And that group created a lot of gravity.

The chief strategic problem for CareerPath centered on what to charge for job listings. In 1996, general search sites like Yahoo! and Lycos and direct jobs-market competitors such as Monster.com were taking listings for free in an effort to build up their job databases. But following that approach would actually undermine the core business of CareerPath's parent companies. After some discussion, CareerPath's leaders decided that CareerPath could post any job listed in one of the parents' papers for free. CareerPath, however, could not take any Internet-only listings.

This decision meant that CareerPath could not easily expand beyond the scope of the newspapers' original business. Companies that wanted to list jobs exclusively on-line simply went to other Web sites that did not carry the CareerPath restriction. As a result, its competitors were able to build their job listings quickly to critical mass. And once they reached critical mass, they could begin charging. They structured their prices so that on-line listings still cost less than advertising in the newspaper.

CareerPath finally threw off its on-line listing restriction in 1997, when even its parents realized that unless it was freed from the interests of the newspapers, it would cede the on-line market to start-ups like CareerMosaic and Monster.com. Today, CareerPath thrives as one of the top on-line contenders, but it does not dominate, as it should have, given the head start it had in job listings.

The CareerPath example demonstrates that even a separate unit alone cannot easily escape the gravitational pull of the old ways of doing business. By giving CareerPath a separate incorporation and access to their job listings, the newspapers felt they had granted the new entity an insurmountable advantage over other start-ups. Yet because the board wanted to protect the interests of the existing print businesses, they devised policies that all but negated CareerPath's initial advantage.

To create an Internet business that will succeed—or at least one that is not doomed to fail—companies must align three aspects of an Internet venture: funding, organization, and leadership. All three must support a single objective.

There is no one correct answer as to how an Internet venture should be funded, what its organization should be, or who should lead it. However, among traditional companies that have made a success of their Internet ventures, three distinct models exist (see Figure 1):

	Wholesale transformation	Risk balancing	Venture participation
Description	Realignment of the entire business around electronic commerce	Creating an Internet business separate from the rest of the organization	Formation of a venture capital group to fund several different Internet businesses
Who should use	Companies who believe most or all of their business will one day be done electronically	Companies with customers distributed between technology optimists and pessimists	Companies with a complex compilation of business units
Benefits	Companies that commit early to this strategy emerge as more powerful industry players	Risk is spread and early adopters are served without jeopardizing traditional business	Use currently profitable business to fund a future Internet position
Pitfalls	Investors, customers, or employees may rebel	Rewards are shared and brand erosion is possible	Company-owned venture groups can be limited by culture or tradition

Source: Forrester Research, Inc.

Figure 1 Three Proven Models for Internet Ventures

1. **Wholesale transformation**—in which the company's leaders decide to turn the traditional company into an Internet-centered company.

2. **Risk balancing**—by which a company invests together with venture capitalists or other companies in order to mitigate the effects that start-up costs can have on the traditional company's income statement.

3. **Venture participation**—in which a company sets up a separate venture capital unit that will compete on equal footing with other, independent venture groups.

Next, we'll look at how each of these each of these models works to align funding, organization, and leadership—and how some traditional companies have used them to succeed in the battle against the start-ups. We'll examine which types of companies do best with each model and identify the common pitfalls.

WHOLESALE TRANSFORMATION

Some traditional companies have realigned their entire business around electronic commerce. For these companies, the Internet is not merely a sales channel or a marketing venue—it is a way to improve their competitive position. These companies envision that most or even all of their business will one day be done electronically. They believe that the traditional business will fade and that the future of their industry lies in electronic commerce. Their mission is to get there first, be the best, and emerge as a larger and more powerful player in their industry.

Companies that pursue wholesale transformation expect the Internet to cause changes in the revenue mix. In fact, they often drive these changes themselves. They engage in what Forrester calls *proactive destruction*—tearing down some sacred aspects of the traditional business to make way for the new (see Figure 2).

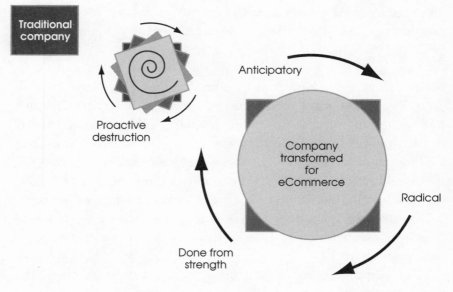

Source: Forrester Research, Inc.

Figure 2 Companies Must Reinvent Themselves with Proactive Destruction

The key to using proactive destruction effectively is to undertake a change that is anticipatory, not reactive. In other words, companies must begin shifting their businesses to the Internet before it is strictly necessary—while the existing businesses are healthy. Proactive destruction brings radical changes, including new pricing structures, sales channels, and customer targets. Because of this, it creates a significant amount of internal and external conflict, and in the short run it sometimes hurts revenues and profits. Navigating these challenges requires nothing short of enormously courageous leadership.

Intuit's transition of TurboTax from a shrink-wrapped software product to a Web-based service is a good example of an effective wholesale transformation. It illustrates the challenges that a company faces in this approach. Intuit entered the tax preparation business in 1993, when it acquired ChipSoft, a San Diego–based company. In the years between 1993 and 1996, Intuit built a dominant position in individual tax preparation for both federal and state income taxes. In fact, by 1996, the company had more than a 75 percent market share in tax preparation software, selling some two million copies of TurboTax through retail stores at a suggested price of $35 apiece.

Not only did consumers buy the TurboTax software, they bought a new release every year to be sure they filed taxes correctly according to the most recent laws. This makes the TurboTax business something of an annuity. For retailers, Turbo Tax drives store traffic—people must go to the store to buy the software in tax season. Retailers would often cut their own margins in order to lower the retail price of TurboTax, hoping to draw in consumers to whom they could sell other software packages and computer peripherals.

Despite the fact that the TurboTax business was a robustly healthy software business in 1996, Intuit began to move it onto the Web (see Figure 3).

According to Larry Wolfe, senior VP of the Tax Product Division, "In the late part of 1995 and early 1996, Intuit entered a period of reflection. We did a serious rethink of who we were and what we were all about." In part, this reflection must have been in

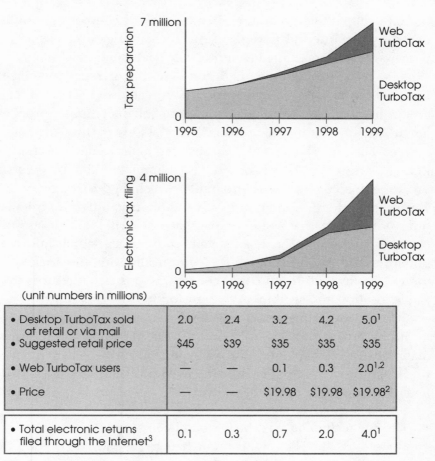

(unit numbers in millions)

	1995	1996	1997	1998	1999
• Desktop TurboTax sold at retail or via mail	2.0	2.4	3.2	4.2	5.0[1]
• Suggested retail price	$45	$39	$35	$35	$35
• Web TurboTax users	—	—	0.1	0.3	2.0[1,2]
• Price	—	—	$19.98	$19.98	$19.98[2]
• Total electronic returns filed through the Internet[3]	0.1	0.3	0.7	2.0	4.0[1]

1. Forrester estimate.
2. For FY 1999 Intuit expects a three- to four-fold expansion of Web TurboTax due to making 1040EZ filing free to users with incomes of $20,000 or less.
3. Electronic filing includes 1040 forms filed via dial-in from Desktop TurboTax as well as forms filed online with Web TurboTax.

Source: Forrester Research, Inc.

Figure 3   Intuit Moves TurboTax to the Web

reaction to the collapse of Intuit's proposed merger with Microsoft that year. However, it was catalyzed principally by a recognition of the importance of the Internet, which started with Kleiner Perkins venture capitalist John Doerr, who sits on Intuit's board, and continued through CEO Scott Cook and president Bill Harris all the way down through the organization. In addition, the company was influenced by the Internal Revenue Service's stated goal of having 80 percent of tax returns filed electronically by the year 2007.

Two initiatives came from Intuit's period of reflection. First, Intuit would aim to make its products available to customers anytime, anywhere. Second, it would move the job of computer processing in its applications away from PC desktops to Internet-based servers. This would enable the company to make updates to its software in one central location. It also eliminated the very costly process of loading a software program— which, in the case of TurboTax, included more than thirty-five thousand different calculations—onto disks that would be packaged and shipped, along with manuals, to stores. Instead, consumers could transfer their information over the Internet and file electronically with the click of a mouse. On its end, Intuit could collect millions of tax returns in a single location and send them directly to the IRS.

In retrospect, this strategy sounds so logical that the company would have to embrace it with enthusiasm. Yet wholesale transformation causes significant disturbances in a business—and Intuit was no exception. According to Bill Harris, Intuit faced four main challenges in moving to the Internet. To make the move, Intuit had to:

- **Change technology**. TurboTax had been written to run on Windows desktops. The application had to be moved to a UNIX operating system so that it could be run at a large scale on the Web site. After all, desktop TurboTax only processed one tax return at a time, but Web TurboTax would handle millions of concurrent filers. Familiar with all the pitfalls of technology transitions, Intuit expected this would to be its most serious challenge. In fact, Harris says, it was the easiest part of the transformation.

- **Develop a new business model**. At retail, Intuit sells software licenses for $35 each, yet on the Web Intuit would charge consumers $19.98 to prepare their tax returns. Because each copy of desktop TurboTax was used to file two tax returns, the company could make the case that it wasn't actually a price cut. But it sure looks like one. To generate additional revenues, Intuit would take advertising and transaction fees from other businesses that sold to consumers via its Web site. Costs changed, too. Harris explains, "The software business had always been characterized by high fixed costs and low variable ones. But once we moved to the Web, that pattern became even more extreme. We found ourselves making huge investments in data-center technology that would have to be useful for three to five years."

- **Become a service provider**. Intuit was, at its core, a product company. Yet on the Web, it had to act as a service organization. Intuit had tried before to operate a service business in bill payment, but it sold that unit, Intuit Services, to CheckFree. It wasn't clear whether the company could succeed at services. "Becoming a service organization challenged us culturally, since we were fundamentally a product company," Harris says. "Each year, we would run like crazy to build this grand product and get it onto the golden master [disk]. Then the whole organization would collapse from exhaustion and collectively go on vacation." Becoming a service organization meant that Intuit would have to be steady as well as fast. "We were proud of being nimble. After all, we got out an update to our product on time every twelve months—that's almost unheard of in the software business. Once we became a service business, though, our annual cycles looked like an anachronism. We had to be up and running all the time."

- **Partner with other companies**. As a Web service provider, Intuit could no longer exist as a stand-alone supplier with control over every aspect of its business. To serve consumers on-line, Intuit would have to partner with other businesses, including financial service suppliers, media concerns, and technology companies. According to Harris, this has proven to be the most difficult challenge of all. "It has been tough to teach the organization that it is okay to depend on others, especially when partners don't come through sometimes. But we realize that even with the disappointments, we can get further, faster, with partners than by being on our own."

In addition to those four challenges, Intuit had to confront one of the central tenets of its product business—the belief that customer feedback should guide the company's decisions. Harris says, "Taking customer research seriously is what got us 80 percent or better market share in every market we served. We asked customers what they wanted, and doggedly we tried to supply it."

But customer research would fail as a means to understand the Internet transition. This is one of the rare times when companies have to lead consumers. When Intuit went out and asked customers in 1996 whether they would put their personal financial information on a Web site, the answer was a resounding no. "It was not just a 'no,' it was a 'Hell No!'" says Harris. "No! No! No! . . . Yet here we are today, with over 1.5 million personal financial portfolios on our Web site."

How did Intuit make this difficult transition? In essence, through its period of reflection and discussion, Intuit's leaders *chose* to take the company in that direction. "We realized that to be first and best we had to be fast. We decided, let's invest, let's show up early," says Harris. "We built our Internet business on the basis of a theoretical construct that flew in the face of all the customer evidence."

Organizationally, companies that pursue a wholesale transformation usually avoid separating the Internet business from other groups. More often, they infuse the entire existing organization with a new mission: move to the Internet. It is not uncommon to see explicit Internet-related goals within every organizational unit. In the information technology group, for example, a typical metric might include the percentage of transactions handled electronically, while the marketing group aims to get a certain number of existing customers to register on the Web site. Sharing and measuring the goal of transformation unifies employees.

During its transformation, Intuit minimized internal conflict between the Web business and the desktop one by organizing around customers, not technology. The engineers working on Turbo-Tax desktop worked alongside those testing TurboTax Web. "We used the same code base and feature design for both products, so it just makes sense to have them working together," says Wolfe. In addition, the company articulated clearly and often that both businesses matter. The only way to fund the growing Internet business was to operate a healthy desktop business during the transition. Bill Harris sums it up this way: "It is the natural desire of humans to see the world in simple terms—black or white, this or that. We are continually reminding ourselves that both Internet and non-Internet activities are vital. We have to do both well."

Funding a transformation involves a high level of risk and courage on the part of existing shareholders. The CEO must convince the board of directors and shareholders that the future of their company lies on the Internet, and he or she must explain that making this transformation will be costly in the short run. The CEO must outline the potential gains from this bold move—expanding market share, perhaps, or cutting costs dramatically. But in the end, a company's owners must be comfortable with the risk that the transformation entails—and it is not at all uncommon for a traded stock to suffer in the near term as wary investors exit.

In the case of Lands' End, another company in the midst of wholesale transformation, a concentration of ownership in the hands of the founder, Gary Comer, has been an advantage. Those who know him describe Comer as a gadgeteer and a Web enthusiast, with a high-speed T1 Internet connection at home. Comer's personal interest in technology explains in part why Lands' End, which was essentially a mom-and-pop catalog operation through the 1970s, is emerging as a leader in electronic commerce—accounting for, by Forrester's estimate, 10 percent of all Internet apparel sales in 1998.

Lands' End's commitment to wholesale transformation did not begin, as Intuit's had, with a focused period of introspection and strategy setting. Instead, Lands' End arrived at the Web through a series of experimental efforts that ranged from putting kiosks in malls, to setting up shop on America Online in 1992, to a Web site launch in 1995—a year when most companies didn't even have a registered Internet domain name. In the beginning, Lands' End viewed its Web site more as a community-building effort than as a sales channel. But when it started selling overstock successfully on

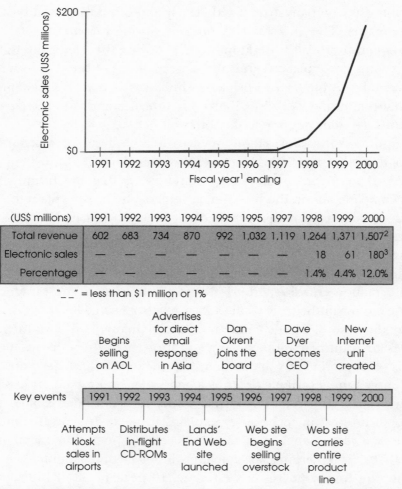

(US$ millions)	1991	1992	1993	1994	1995	1995	1997	1998	1999	2000
Total revenue	602	683	734	870	992	1,032	1,119	1,264	1,371	1,507[2]
Electronic sales	—	—	—	—	—	—	—	18	61	180[3]
Percentage	—	—	—	—	—	—	—	1.4%	4.4%	12.0%

"_ _" = less than $1 million or 1%

1. Lands' End's fiscal year ends January 31. Fiscal year 1999 reflects mainly calendar year.
2. Forrester estimate based on previous three years CAGR.
3. Forrester estimate.

Source: Forrester Research, Inc.

Figure 4   Lands' End's Journey to Electronic Commerce

the site in 1997, the company began to see the Internet in a new light (see Figure 4).

In mid-1997, Lands' End invited Dan Okrent, then chief editor of Time, Inc. New Media, to join the board of directors. At age forty-nine, Okrent was the young blood on the Lands' End board, which was composed of Comer's longtime associates—most of them now over seventy years old. While he didn't have a background in catalog operations or apparel, Okrent did have a unique perspective on communications. Here was the former editor of *Life* magazine, a significant intellectual figure at the world's largest publishing company, giving speeches all over the world about how the Internet would cause the end of print in our lifetime.

At the end of 1997, the Lands' End board and management made an internal commitment to the Internet and stepped up investments in the Web site. Lands' End generated 1 percent of sales electronically in 1997 and 4.5 percent in 1998. It wasn't much in the context of a $1.4 billion business, but the growth rate was astonishing. Overall, though, the company had a bad year in 1998, with disappointing sales and excess inventory that had to be written off. Toward the end of the year, Lands' End replaced CEO Mike Smith with Dave Dyer from J Crew.

Dyer cut the flab out of Lands' End, slashing 11 percent of the salaried staff and replacing many others. It was not business as usual. In addition to bringing in new management in merchandising and product design, Dyer hired Bill Bass, who had been director of Forrester's media and retail research groups as VP of eCommerce. Perhaps most important, Dyer articulated to the entire company that a huge part of its future sales would likely come from the Internet.

Like Intuit, Lands' End could envision clear benefits to moving most of its business on-line. As Bass puts it, "Our single largest operating cost is printing and mailing out a quarter of a billion catalogs each year. It's 43 percent of our operating cost. The Internet has the potential to cut that cost dramatically." Yet to gain these benefits, Lands' End has faced both internal and external challenges.

Internally, the biggest issue has been generating support from all the different departments. The IT organization had always focused on inventory control and billing records. Now, IT had to build Web pages and learn how to connect the Web site to the telephone system so on-line customers could get help if they needed it. The creative department excelled at laying out pictures and words on paper. Now, it had to design for the landscape of computer screens. Merchandisers worried that the Internet would cause prices to fall—and that Lands' End's superior clothing construction could get overlooked in a world of price-comparison engines.

To address the internal challenge, Lands' End adopted a dual reporting structure. All members of the Internet team report jointly to Bass and to their traditional department head. Although having two bosses is not always easy, as Bass points out, "If the Internet is really going to be as central to the business as we believe it will be, we want to organize in a way that lets the whole company morph as the transition occurs. We don't want to end up in a situation where there are a bunch of people isolated in a catalog unit that end up lacking Internet skills because we didn't bring them along." Having a shared reporting structure gives the departments ownership of the Web effort and creates evangelists throughout the company. Bass explains, "If I do my job right, I'll be out of a job in four years. We won't need an Internet unit, because the whole company will be an Internet company."

Externally, the key question has revolved around the company's relationships with it two sets of customers—on-line and off-line. Since the first Web site sales were focused on overstock, the implicit assumption was that catalog customers were primary and on-line buyers, secondary. In fact, when Bass arrived, the company had the practice of taking off the Web site any product that was selling briskly through the catalog. Since printed catalogs in the field couldn't be changed, Lands' End effectively held the inventory of popular items for its catalog consumers. Now, "It's first come, first serve. We leave products up for sale on-line until they're out of stock, just as we do for catalog items," says Bass.

In fact, the pendulum seems to be swinging the other way, with on-line customers receiving service that Lands' End simply cannot bring to its paper catalog consumers. It is so much easier to bring a product to market on a Web site than it is to print a catalog and mail it that, in a few cases, products that do not appear in any Land's End catalog have been offered on the Web. Yet even if Internet sales for Lands' End grow to $200 or $300 million dollars fairly quickly, the company still does over a billion dollars in catalog sales. It has not lost sight of its more mainstream consumers.

In both the Intuit and the Lands' End examples, clear leadership has been the single most important factor driving the success of the transformation. The experiences of these two very different companies offer several important lessons about what leaders must provide in order to effect a transformation.

- **Shared vision**. Everyone in the company must understand that the company is moving its business to the Internet. Intuit got there consciously, through a period of reflection, while Lands' End arrived as a product of many years of experimentation with technology.

- **No separation**. Internet operations in transformational companies are blended with traditional operations. In Intuit's case, Internet efforts belong entirely to the business units, which are organized along customer lines. In the case of Lands' End, Internet operations are owned by functional departments such as IT and merchandising—with the clear expectation that the Internet unit will no longer be a separate entity as the on-line business grows.

- **Customers are customers**. Intuit and Lands' End assign equal value to customers of their traditional business and consumers of their new Web-based offerings. They may try to persuade consumers to move more quickly to the Internet, but they do not abandon slower-moving consumers. Nor do they penalize more advanced ones.

RISK BALANCING

For some companies, a wholesale transformation is not only undesirable, it isn't even possible. Companies whose consumer Technographics profile shows a high percentage of mainstream or laggard consumers face a situation where many, perhaps even most, of their consumers will never do business with them on-line. Yet such companies always serve some early adopters. The challenge is to serve on-line consumers well when the bulk of the company's management attention is legitimately focused elsewhere.

Often companies with a broad array of different consumer Technographics groups have correspondingly complex organizations that cover many different brands, target consumers, and even countries. The sheer size of some consumer companies makes it very tough to operate an Internet business from within. All the systems that yield predictability—methodical management review of investments, annual planning processes, and average profitability targets, for example—weigh against the effective management of an Internet business. In short, for large and complex businesses, it is nearly impossible to reposition the entire company around electronic commerce. And it would not be appropriate.

Companies of this sort are most often owned by a large number of relatively risk-averse investors. These are, after all, the blue chip consumer companies—the ones that supply basic consumer goods and services and deliver dependable performance to pension funds and widows. Funding an Internet venture that serves only part of the customer base and might generate huge losses in the near term is out of the question.

These companies do best if they separate their Internet business from the rest of the organization. Separating makes it possible to attract funding and leadership more appropriate to an Internet venture. It also frees the Internet unit to address market opportunities that would have been taboo within the larger parent organization.

Consider, for example, how Disney used risk balancing as a means to gain a leading Internet media position with GO network.

In 1994, Paul Allen, one of the original founders of Microsoft and now a prominent individual investor, funded a company in Seattle called StarWave, with the mission of building new Internet media properties around sports and entertainment. With experienced media executive Mike Slade at the helm, StarWave had the almost unbelievable good fortune to license the ESPN Sports brand from ABC for use on the Web. Thus was ESPN SportsZone formed.

In 1996, Disney bought ABC and along with it, television's ESPN. Until this time, the StarWave/ESPN deal had been purely a brand licensing arrangement, but now Disney insisted on making ESPN SportsZone a joint venture. According to Harry Motro, who ran CNN Interactive at the time, "There was this big dance that went on. Disney could pull the ESPN brand from StarWave, and that gave Disney a good position from which to negotiate." At one point, Slade approached Motro about using CNN brands, and possibly Time-Warner's *Sports Illustrated* brand instead of ESPN.[2] But in the end, Disney ended up buying a half ownership in StarWave with an option to buy the rest.

Meanwhile, at Disney's corporate office, Jake Winebaum was building an on-line presence for Disney's many valuable traditional media properties. Winebaum reported directly to Disney's CEO Michael Eisner, and this made it easier for Disney than for most companies to build some effective Internet businesses—including the number one kids' site, Disney.com. On the whole, compared with other traditional media companies, Disney was doing well. Yet the company lacked a really big hit on the level of a Yahoo! or an America Online. Enter Infoseek, one of the original contenders in the race for search engine dominance. Through a combination of inaccurate positioning as a superior technology player and underaggressive leadership, Infoseek had ended up with a depressed stock price and falling market share. In mid-1997, Infoseek ousted CEO Robin Johnson and brought in Harry Motro from CNN Interactive.

Motro set about strengthening Infoseek's site and its brand in anticipation of the moment he knew was coming—when every major media company from NBC to Time Warner to Disney would wake up and wonder why they weren't running Yahoo! Then, they would all go looking for a search engine. There would be Infoseek, alongside Lycos and AltaVista, as the last chances for traditional media companies to become serious contenders in the Internet business. Motro worked doggedly to raise Infoseek's valuation, and he succeeded—from $100 million when he joined to over $1 billion by the time negotiations with Disney began.

Disney's objective was to parlay its strong niche positions in Disney.com and ESPN.com into a dominant portal play. Yet Disney knew that if it exercised its right to buy the rest of StarWave, taking away the possibility of issuing public stock, it would never be able to recruit the kind of aggressive executive talent that is required in an Internet company. In addition, if Disney were to try to build from scratch a branded search site with all the features then offered by Yahoo! and America Online, it would take more than a year and cost $100 million or more.

So Disney reached an agreement whereby it gave StarWave, whose closest comparable competitor, CBS Sportsline, was valued at over $700 million at the time, to Infoseek. In return, Disney got 43 percent of Infoseek and warrants that gave Disney the right to bring its voting share of the company to 51 percent. In addition, Disney paid Infoseek $130 million in cash and notes, and Infoseek agreed to spend $165 million on marketing through Disney's TV shows, theme parks, and movies (see Figure 5).

Infoseek formed a new network, called GO, whose content spanned Infoseek search, ABC news, ESPN sports, and Disney family fare. At its launch, GO network was immediately among the top five Internet properties. It was the only one owned in large part by a traditional company.

Let's look at the benefits of Disney's risk-balancing strategy. By sharing ownership as it built its Internet businesses, Disney accomplished several objectives:

- **Avoid start-up costs**. Both StarWave and Infoseek incurred losses in the tens of millions when building their businesses. Yet

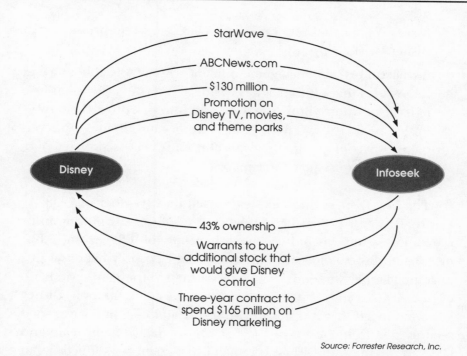

Source: Forrester Research, Inc.

Figure 5 The Disney/Infoseek Deal that Created Go Network

because Disney took minority ownership positions until these Internet businesses became profitable, it recognized only a portion of those losses in the income statements of Disney proper.

- **Control the brands.** While Disney was a minority holder in Star-Wave and then Infoseek, the company always retained the ability to take control. As Motro puts it, "If they were going to put in valuable brands like ESPN and ABC, Disney wanted a path to control. At Infoseek, we still wanted some autonomy while we were launching GO, so the warrants were a good solution for both of us."

- **Support the Internet business completely**. Even though Disney didn't run its principal Internet play in-house, it supported GO through marketing and promotion. Infoseek agreed to pay Disney $165 million over three years. In return, GO got the kind of marketing that money can't usually buy—a feature role in Zoog

Disney TV shows, URLs on Disney packaging, and promotion at Disney World.

- **Attract and retain management talent**. Disney was able to avoid the exodus that often plagues in-house Internet efforts because of its acquisitions. Both StarWave and Infoseek offered plenty of upside to their employees—StarWave because it always offered the prospect of going public, and Infoseek because it had a publicly traded, pure-play Internet stock.

The first Disney/Infoseek deal closed in November of 1998. As I write, Disney is preparing to take control of GO. By putting in its remaining assets, including the other half of ESPN.com, ABC-news.com, disney.com, and family.com, and possibly exercising its warrants, Disney will end up with more than 75 percent ownership of Infoseek. To address the issue of executive compensation, Disney has announced that it will issue a tracking stock—a publicly traded security tied to the assets of GO but whose management team and CEO are shared with Disney. It remains to be seen how effective that strategy will be. While not directly in response to this plan, Winebaum has left Disney and Motro has announced his departure at the end of 1999. One result *is* clear: Disney has a top-five Internet property, and, so far, no other major media company does.

As an Internet strategy, risk balancing is most often found in media companies. Barnesandnoble.com, the *New York Times,* Classified Ventures, and CareerPath.com all chose this strategy—either by combining the investments of several players or by taking the Internet unit partly public. Perhaps one reason this strategy shows up so much in the media industry is that these companies are accustomed to managing a complex maze of ownership relationships. A media colleague once quipped, "No one actually owns the media . . . they all own each other."

As an industry analyst, I can't help wondering why risk balancing does not show up more prominently in other industries, especially retail. Few retailers can afford to fund an Internet start-up adequately—and the venture community is nearly desperate to keep up the pace of successful investment it has enjoyed over the past five years.

The chief disadvantage of balancing the risk is that the reward must then be shared. And it is unquestionably dangerous to lend a well-established brand to an operation that is only partly owned. Yet risk balancing remains far better than the alternative of keeping the Internet business in-house, where it will almost certainly be under-funded and plagued with political infighting. That path invariably results in a second-rate Web site that fails to generate business and erodes a valuable brand in the process.

Contrast the case of Disney with the one chosen by Time Warner, which tried to build its own portal to compete with Yahoo! and America Online. With a stable of magazines that includes *Time, Fortune, Money, Sports Illustrated, People,* and *Entertainment Weekly,* Time Warner arguably had the strongest single content position in the entire media industry—and some of the best brands in every category. For its run at the Internet, Time Warner opted to put all these assets together under a new Internet brand: Pathfinder.

Pathfinder was funded internally and had its own editorial staff. In theory, Pathfinder could draw upon the content produced at the magazines as well. But in practice, complicated internal relation-ships made that difficult. Moreover, Pathfinder struggled to gain brand recognition among consumers. It didn't help that Nissan was actively promoting a sport utility vehicle with the same name.

In 1996, Pathfinder lost more than $10 million by Forrester's estimate—a rate that Don Logan, then CEO of Time Inc., character-ized as giving "new meaning to the term black hole." In addition, Time Warner's established brands, held captive to Pathfinder, were being eclipsed. ESPN and CBSSportsline outperformed *Sports Illus-trated;* while start-up money sites such as *Motley Fool* did better than venerable *Fortune* and *Money.* Only *People,* Time-Warner's most valu-able property of all, was able to hold its own against entertainment competitors lik E! Online.

By the spring of 1999, Time Warner had had enough. It pulled the plug on Pathfinder as a brand and turned its attention to building on its strong category brands and capitalizing on its position in cable television. This strategy will give the company another shot at Internet dominance as broadband networking takes hold.

VENTURE PARTICIPATION

The last model for Internet funding, organization, and leadership is recruiting venture participation, that is, forming a venture capital group to fund several different Internet businesses. The wisdom of this approach lies in the fact that, for most large companies, funding just one Internet venture—their own—is far too risky. Venture capitalists would never dream of pouring their entire fund in a single dotcom.

By forming a venture group that will take a position in ten or fifteen different Internet ventures, a large consumer company can use its current profitable business to fund a future position on the Internet. And these investments need not all be made in dollars. Some ventures may inherit assets or people from the various business units of a larger corporation—business units that, on their own, would benefit from a wholesale transformation. It is important that ventures inheriting assets and people as well as money from the parent company be separately incorporated and managed. Otherwise, even a well-funded offspring will fall prey to other sources of paralysis— lack of leadership, organizational ambivalence, or channel conflict.

A venture structure offers enormous advantages for companies that have a complex compilation of business units. Most important, this structure lets a company measure its performance and compete directly with its channel partners—but in such an arm's-length way that it is relatively easy for management to quell any protest from current shareholders or channel partners. This approach offers larger companies a speed to market that can never be accomplished in an organization where new initiatives require months or years of repetitive communication and acculturation for employees. And it enables the company to acquire Internet know-how from among its stable of initial investments at a later time.

The venture approach to Internet funding can be applied by any consumer company—for it does not exclude other strategies. One of the best examples of this strategy in action is CMG Corporation. CMG was originally a mail-order list company. As luck would have it, CMG developed a Web browser, called BookLink, very early on. For a time, it was the best browser on the market. CMG sold BookLink to America Online for $35 million in 1995 and used that money to form a venture group. Today, CMG's Internet investments include Lycos, Tripod, Engage, and AltaVista, among others.

The main risk in the venture participation approach is that many large companies won't take their own investment strategy seriously enough. Too often, I have seen recent MBAs or corporate dead-enders assigned to do "business development"—and given no specific amount to invest. Companies that want to pursue this strategy must treat the venture group as a fairly autonomous entity. Management of the venture group must be personally invested—as all venture capitalists are—in the portfolio. And the corporation must be careful not to impose limits on the nature of companies the venture group can invest in, lest it create a competitive disadvantage for its own money in the market.

CONCLUSIONS

One of the questions I hear most often from clients is, "How should we organize our Internet effort?" I tell them that there is no right answer—that it depends on a company's consumer Technographics, on the speed and nature of business model change in their industry, and on the ability of the organization to fund Internet set-up costs.

What is consistently true from one company to another is that all the elements of funding, organization, and leadership must align toward the same goal. If they don't, the Internet initiative will almost certainly fail to achieve its objectives. It does no good to create a separate organization if that discrete unit is still tied to the biases of the larger whole. All the funding in the world won't rescue

211

an Internet unit that has to spend half its management time in large-company "think out of the box" meetings.

Traditional companies that have created successful Internet businesses have pursued one of three basic models: wholesale transformation of the existing business into an electronic one; a risk-balancing approach in which a separate unit seeks some outside funding; and a hands-off venture investment approach. In the end, however, all of these approaches require the direct and active support of the CEO. No Internet strategy can succeed without it.

CHAPTER 12

The Will to Win

The battle for Internet consumers is quickly shaping up to be one of the most intensely competitive business wars ever waged. The combination of shifting consumer behavior and new Internet business models has created a do-or-die situation, both for Internet start-up companies and for traditional players in consumer industries.

Internet start-ups must grow at a breathtaking pace to support their investors' expectations. For these newly formed companies, there is no choice but to acquire customers and revenue as fast as possible—and most do so at the cost of ever widening losses. Traditional players must defend their customer base as they try to regear their company around the new business models. In most cases, this makeover requires cutting prices, improving service, and reducing costs faster than ever before. In short, the Internet makes consumer industries far more competitive and dynamic than they were in the past.

As this day-to-day rivalry intensifies, it will become more important to step back and identify the sources of long-term value. Simply running like mad to sign up customers may be rewarded in the short run, particularly since the economies of scale in Internet businesses are so pronounced. Gaining market share, however, is not enough. Internet businesses are not natural monopolies, and there is no rule that states that once a company has acquired its customers, it can relax and go back to pricing above cost. Entry barriers remain low, and the key assets that Internet companies build—brand awareness and technology know-how—can be fumbled away in a single year.

In this harsh environment, companies that intend to thrive in the long run must build a defensible strategic position. In other words, these companies need to build an advantage that other companies do not have in the marketplace. Cutting prices by 50 percent and running Super Bowl advertisements may create huge short-term growth, but it does nothing to secure the future of a company. Having a hot IPO or a high stock price may help, but it won't suffice. The companies that ultimately will win the battle for Internet consumers see now that profitless growth cannot go on forever and simply being "a dotcom" does not constitute a strategic advantage.

As the Internet matures, companies must learn to compete in a world of Dynamic Trade, where the apparent supply to consumers rises and companies must heed the signals of current demand—what consumers want now. Dynamic Trade will make consumer industries more efficient and on the whole less profitable than they were in the past.

The companies that thrive in this environment must build a unique value. One way to do this is to build a brand based on consumer experiences. A projected image, even one that has millions of dollars in marketing budget behind it, won't stand up unless the everyday experiences of consumers on the Internet reinforce the brand. Companies that ignore this truth will find that they're not just wasting half their advertising budget; as John Wanamaker famously asserted, they're wasting all of it.

The only way to build a brand based on consumer experience is to become a master at using consumer demand data. Unglamorous as analyzing data may sound, it holds the key to identifying trends such as increasing apparent supply and volatile current demand. Seat-of-the-pants judgments about whether to produce more or change prices or expand distribution will give way to market responses based on evidence in the Internet Economy. Rather than plan ahead for production and pricing, companies will adjust to market conditions based on information culled from the Web site.

Companies that build a large customer base will be in a considerably better position to spot demand trends than smaller organizations will be. Only organizations that make sufficient investments in technology and sales distribution will be able to generate consumer information on the scale that will be required to respond to demand—and to separate collective demand data from sensitive personal information, which should be kept off-limits for commercial purposes.

In the Internet Economy, success has come quickly to many start-up companies. But staying on top will prove more difficult than many newly minted industry scions may imagine. Companies that survive the test of time must have skills and assets that other companies do not possess and cannot easily copy. Developing experiential brands and mastering the art of measuring and responding to current demand offer two good paths. A third is to own the physical distribution systems upon which all Internet businesses must rely.

In the Internet Economy, only physical distribution is fundamentally a natural monopoly. And for that reason, I believe it will prove to be one of the most valuable, lasting assets that a company can own. This may seem counterintuitive is a time when the fashion is to build "virtual" companies, with few or no physical assets. Yet in a virtual world, everyone must ultimately depend on a few physical distributors.

Cultivating relationships with physical distributors will become more important to manufacturers as sales through retail stores are replaced in part by direct sales over the Internet. Consumers look for the products first at foremost brand sites. As a result, most manufacturers, even those that have never sold direct find themselves hosting their own consumers in search of products. Over time it is becoming more and more absurd in the eyes of consumers not to be able to buy the product that a company makes over its Web site.

To serve consumers and generate enough demand information, most manufacturers will have little choice but to sell direct and also to expand the number of Internet venues selling their products as fast and as far as possible—into the thousands, even millions in some cases. In this environment, negotiating one by one with each

Web site that could carry products or create leads is too time-consuming. Instead, manufacturers need to separate Internet channel partners into tiers that include lead-generating affiliates, physical distribution partners, and the Web sites of traditional retailers.

FOUNDING AND FUNDING

If there is one thing I've learned in my ten years as an industry analyst, it's that the companies that win are usually the ones that want to most. For that reason, I always ask the companies that come through Forrester to introduce themselves and tell me about the two Fs—founding and funding. I ask the same questions of the Internet units of traditional companies that, more recently, have set up appointments to talk about their electronic commerce plans. I want to know who is backing the company and what their goals are; also who is running the company, what experiences led them to form a new company, and what their objectives are.

I have found that when you focus on the "who" rather than the "what" of a new business, the likely winners stand out a mile from the rest of the pack. A meeting I had with Jeff Bezos provides a good illustration of this. I first met Bezos at a coffee shop in Cambridge. This was in 1996, before Amazon.com and its founder became larger than life selling a billion dollars worth of books, music, videos, and more over the Internet. I had never heard of Bezos before this, and neither had most people. We sat down, and Bezos got started on the the two Fs. And here is what he told me.

Bezos had been in finance, but realized that the Internet was going to change consumer businesses somehow. So, he went systematically through all the different categories of consumer goods, thinking about which would be the best, first product to sell on-line. He decided to sell books because, after he had calculated the cost to take orders and pick, pack, and ship products, he concluded that books offered the best value-to-cost ratio. So, even though he had no experience in the book industry, Bezos raised some seed financing and founded Amazon.com as a bookseller.

Company	Reach (%)	Unique visitors (000)	Type of company
Blue Mountain Arts	16.3	10,089	●
Amazon.com	16.0	9,933	○
eBay	13.3	8,227	○
Cnet Software Download Services	7.6	4,709	●
Barnesandnoble.com	7.0	4,330	●
MuPoints	5.6	3,491	○
CDNOW	5.4	3,345	○
ValuPage	5.2	3,224	○
FreeShop	4.4	2,719	○
CoolSavings	4.1	2,543	○
Ticketmaster	4.1	2,512	●
Columbia House	3.6	2,257	●
Beyond.com	3.4	2,104	○
Classifieds2000	3.3	2,022	○
BMG Music Service	3.2	1,951	●
Egreetings	3.1	1,949	○
priceline.com	3.1	1,922	○
Egghead.com	3.1	1,907	●
Dell	2.9	1,765	●
Buy.com	2.6	1,594	○
CNet Commerce Services	2.5	1,571	●
LowestFare.com	2.4	1,504	●
OnSale	2.4	1,476	○
CarPoint	2.1	1,309	●
uBid	2.1	1,308	○
123Greetings.com	2.1	1,287	○
Spree.com	2.0	1,229	○
eToys	1.9	1,163	○
QVC	1.8	1,086	●
BigStar	1.7	1,053	○
Fingerhut	1.7	1,029	●
Lands' End	1.6	1,017	●
ShopNow.com sites	1.6	921	○
drugstore.com	1.5	910	○
Autoweb.com	1.5	905	○
Reel.com	1.5	899	○
Music Boulevard	1.4	891	○
CDW	1.4	869	●
First Auction	1.4	847	○
Netmarket	1.4	842	●

● Established company   ○ Internet start-up

Source: Media Metrix, Inc.

Figure 1 Top 40 Shopping Sites by Reach and Unique Visitors for May 1999

As we drank our coffee, Bezos went through a very rigorous discussion about the current and potential economics of on-line book selling. He used no slides, no handouts, and no public relations support. Only himself, his idea, and his analysis of the situation. And it was clear to me then, as it is to me now, that no matter what happened to Amazon.com in the near term, Jeff Bezos would probably end up as a winner—not just because he was smart, but because he wanted to win.

When I am asked which type of company is most likely to win on the Internet—traditional companies or dotcoms—I can only say that nothing about either heritage guarantees Internet success. Already the top Web sites in every category as measured by consumer traffic include a healthy mix of new and established companies (see Figure 1).

The past is not what will drive the future.

Winners will align their organization, funding, and leadership around the Internet Economy and Dynamic Trade. They will set aside or manage diversions such as potential channel conflict. They will fund their Internet operations fully enough to create revenue growth momentum—and they will find this funding from patient sources that can be comfortable with the risk of generating losses in the near term. The winners will assign or recruit the best people to electronic commerce and give them enough authority to challenge the old ways of doing business—and they'll do it quickly. In the end, the companies that win the battle for Internet consumers will be the ones that really want to.

APPENDIX

Technographics Methodology

During the last two years, Forrester has surveyed more than 250,000 North American households to understand their levels of receptiveness to technology-based products and services. Our annual Technographics Benchmark Surveys of more than 100,000 North American households form the foundation of this research. These surveys measure ownership and use of TVs, PCs, video games, telephones, and on-line technologies as well as print, radio, television, and Internet consumption habits. Results include cross-references against demographic variables like age, gender, income, geography, and family size. In addition to consumers' general attitudes toward technology, the surveys measure opinions about media and entertainment, the Internet, and on-line transactions.

To supplement this research, we conduct four surveys per year to track data on technology penetration and marketing issues surrounding electronic commerce, new media, and on-line financial services. Each of these secondary surveys generates seven thousand to ten thousand responses.

This book draws on data from Forrester's Technographics '99 Field Study of nearly one hundred thousand North American households. The data is weighted to demographically represent the North American population. Statistics based on this data are accurate to ±1 percent.

FORRESTER'S TECHNOGRAPHICS SEGMENTATION AND SCALE

What helps us determine consumers' technology receptiveness is Forrester's unique Technographics Segmentation: *a model designed to categorize consumers based on their attitudes, motivations, and abilities to use or acquire technology.*

To populate this segmentation, Forrester developed a series of fifteen attributes, called the Technographics Scale. Respondents rate those attributes on a scale of 1 to 10, depending on how strongly they agree or disagree with each attribute. Multivariate statistical techniques, such as factor analysis, cluster analysis, and discriminant analysis, generate the ten distinct consumer segments that form the Technographics Segmentation (see Figure 1).

The segments derived from the Technographics Scale can be viewed along three axes: attitude toward technology, income, and primary motivation. The first divides consumers into two major

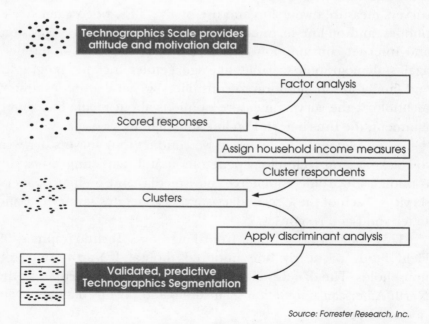

Source: Forrester Research, Inc.

Figure 1   How We Generate the Technographics Segmentation

camps: technology optimists and pessimists. Technology optimists believe that new technology will make their lives simpler, while technology pessimists show little interest in using technology for needs or desires that can be satisfied through traditional methods.

Technology optimists and pessimists can be further split into roughly equal groups by their household income: (1) high-income consumers, with annual household incomes exceeding $40,000 for families or $25,000 for singles; and (2) low-income consumers, with incomes that fall below these cutoffs.

The Technographics Scale then categorizes consumers into one of three primary motivations based on consumers' strongest needs: career, family, or entertainment. Career motivation represents the need to get ahead or feel important at work; family motivations are associated with the need to nurture or provide care; and entertain-

Enabling Tools	
Technographics Scale	Fifteen statements respondents rate on a scale of 1 to 10 that can be incorporated into a client's proprietary research. This permits our clients to analyze their own research by the three Technographics axes.
Focus group screener	Clients can use this screener in their own focus group research to recruit respondents based on their Technographics Segment. These respondents can then be used to test marketing messages and conduct usability research.
Predictive database modeling	This tool allows enables clients to score customer databases for technology optimism and other factors. Forrester can develop algorithms for clients by building CHAID functions, using data consistent with the Technographics Field Study databases and clients' customer records, like age, income, or gender.
Partnerships	
Mediamark Research (MRI)	Enables clients to analyze their research by the Technographics axes. MRI has embedded the Technographics Scale into its semiannual Field Studies.
NPD and Greenfield Research	Resampling respondents of Technographics Field Studies enables clients to select a sample based on specific Technographics attributes and append a proprietary survey to the Technographics Field Studies.
Experian	Database enhancement and direct mail campaigns based on Technographics enable clients to analyze their customer databases and target offers to prospect households. Forrester and Experian have partnered to score all U.S. households for Technographics and specific activity and technology usage.
Plaza Research	Recruitment and facilitation of Technographics focus groups provide clients with the highest-quality recruitment and state-of-the-art facilities in 12 metropolitan areas in the United States. Plaza Research has programmed the screener into their CATI system.

The above services are available to Forrester's Technographic Service clients

Source: Forrester Research, Inc.

Figure 2 Technographics Tools and Partnerships

ment motivations correspond with the need to have fun. The primary motivation axis helps marketers to develop successful messages once they've used the attitude and income axes to identify receptive consumers.

We believe that the Technographics Segmentation and Scale can help marketers integrate technology attitudes and motivations into their strategies. Our extensive field research and predictive database modeling can help businesses of different scopes in a variety of industries to: (1) map the demographic profiles of consumer segments for optimism/pessimism; (2) market on-line offerings to customers most likely to change their behavior; and (3) build a business case for introducing new products or services.

The real value of Technographics depends on a company's ability to apply it in making business decisions. Forrester has developed special tools and established partnerships to help clients use Technographics in the most valuable way (see Figure 2).

ENDNOTES

INTRODUCTION

1. Research enthusiasts can turn to the appendix for an overview of Forrester's methodology and information about how Technographics links to other consumer data from Mediamark Research, Media Metrix, and Experian.

2. Unless otherwise noted, consumer data presented in *Now or Never* comes from Forrester's Technographics 1999 Field Study.

3. Thanks to Joe Liemandt, CEO of Trilogy Software, who first told me this story.

CHAPTER 3

1. Source: American Airlines.

2. Source: MRI Fall 1998 Report, All Rights Reserved.

3. Source: MRI Fall 1998 Report, All Rights Reserved.

4. Source: MRI Fall 1998 Report, All Rights Reserved.

CHAPTER 4

1. Source: MRI Fall 1998 Report, All Rights Reserved.

2. Source: MRI Fall 1998 Report, All Rights Reserved.

3. Source: "Investors Grade Online Brokers," Forrester Research, 1999.

4. Source: Fidelity Investments.

5. Source: Harvard Business School Case #N9–899–116 "The Knot."

6. Source: "The Knot."

CHAPTER 5

1. Source: MRI Fall 1998 Report, All Rights Reserved.

2. Source: MRI Fall 1998 Report, All Rights Reserved.

CHAPTER 6

1. Source: W. A. Dean & Associates.

2. Source: International Customer Service Association.

3. Source: Direct Marketing Association.

4. Source: The Food Marketing Institute.

CHAPTER 7

1. Source: Airlines Reporting Corporation.

2. Source: Airlines Reporting Corporation.

3. Microsoft had agreed to merge with Intuit at that time, a deal that fell through because of rising fears at Microsoft that such a merger would hasten an investigation by the Justice Department.

4. Eric Schonfeld, "Schwab Puts It All Online: Schwab Bet the Farm on Low-Cost Trading and in the Process Invented a New Kind of Brokerage," *Fortune,* December 7, 1998.

CHAPTER 8

1. For an excellent article on experiential branding, see Joseph Pine II and James Gilmore, "Welcome to the Experience Economy," *Harvard Business Review,* July 1, 1998.

2. Source: Kimberly Blanton, "Fleet Mortgage Settles Loan Bias Suit, Will Pay $4M to Minority Customers, End Justice Probe," *Boston Globe,* May 8, 1996.

CHAPTER 9

1. "Coax" means coaxial cable, which is the type generally used in cable systems today.

2. Asynchronous transfer mode, or ATM, chops up network traffic such as voice, data, and video into smaller units, called cells. The cells are all the same size, which allows them to be switched as individual units through the network. Different cells take different paths to reach their destination, so they have to be reassembled at the other end. This reassembly happens so fast that a consumer never notices that the information was scrambled during transmission.

CHAPTER 10

1. In fact, channel conflict is such a sensitive issue that some identifying characteristics of the companies whose stories I will tell in this chapter have been changed to protect their privacy.

2. Source: MRI Fall 1998 report, All Rights Reserved.

CHAPTER 11

1. See chapter 7 for background on the competitive dynamics in classified ads.

2. Time Warner, owner of *Sports Illustrated,* was then merging with CNN.

INDEX